MEMORY FEVER

Camino del Sol
A Latina and Latino Literary Series

Memory Fever

A Journey Beyond *El Paso del Norte*

Ray Gonzalez

The University of Arizona Press

Tucson

The University of Arizona Press
Copyright © 1993 by Ray Gonzalez. First University of Arizona
Press paperbound edition 1999.
∞ This book is printed on acid-free, archival-quality paper.
Manufactured in the United States of America
04 03 02 01 00 99   6 5 4 3 2 1

Grateful acknowledgment is made to the following publications,
where some of these essays, in an earlier form, first appeared:
"The Third Eye of the Lizard," in *The Guadalupe Review*; "White
Sands" in *I.E. Magazine* and *Readings from the Red Earth* (Colorado
Council for the Arts, 1989); "Peace Grove" in *Tonantzin*; "Without
Discovery" in *Without Discovery: A Native Response to Columbus*
(Broken Moon Press, 1992); "The Active Poet" in *Nova Quarterly*
and *Tracks in the Snow: Essays by Colorado Poets* (Mesilla Press,
1987); "Mama Menudo" in *El Universal*; "With Neruda in the
Desert" in *Mid American Review*. Thanks, too, to the White Pine
Press for permission to quote from *The Stones of Chile*, by Pablo
Neruda (translated by Dennis Maloney, 1986).

Library of Congress Cataloging-in-Publication Data

González, Ray.
Memory fever : a journey beyond El Paso del Norte / Ray Gonzalez.
    p.   cm. — (Camino del sol)
Originally published: Seattle : Broken Moon Press, c1993.
ISBN 0-8165-2011-9 (pbk.)
1. González, Ray.   2. Mexican Americans—Texas—El Paso—Social
life and customs.   3. Authors, American—20th century—
Biography.   4. Mexican American authors—Texas—Biography.
5. El Paso (Tex.)—Social life and customs.   I. Title.   II. Series.
PS3557.O476Z472   1999   99-30986
811'.54—dc21   CIP
[B]

British Library Cataloguing-in-Publication Data
A catalogue record for this book is available from the
British Library.

CONTENTS

INTRODUCTION

I have not lived in El Paso since 1979, but I have returned to my hometown many times. Family reunions, literary conferences, and the need to immerse myself briefly in the power of the Southwest landscape have brought me back. Yet it seems that every time I visit I notice changes in the environment of the area and the rapid urban decay of the El Paso–Juárez metropolis. As I land at the airport, I am hit immediately with stark visions of disappearing deserts. From my plane window it is easy to spot miles of flat desert that is being scarred by new housing developments. Dirt roads in the distance that once led to isolated canyons and arroyos are now intersected by a new freeway or the latest maze of pipeline meandering toward the horizon. The drive to my mother's house by one of my sisters includes conversation on the growing crime rate in the city and the fact that our old neighborhood now contains houses with iron bars on the windows, something we never knew as children.

I go stand by the Rio Grande River, hoping it is one source of my past that has not been transformed. As it moves along imaginary borders, it runs a cycle from completely dry to nearly overflowing. The farther south it goes, the more polluted it becomes. As I arrive for my latest visit, I know I can drive to the Mesilla Valley of southern New Mexico to see the river's steady flow as I have always remembered it. When I make notes on these vast changes, I promise myself I will write about them someday. I am the only member of my immediate family to have left the desert and may see it in ways they can't. My love and longing for the Southwest have not diminished, but my view of it has been greatly transformed over the past twenty years. It is nothing new for a writer to return home and find things have changed. It is perhaps the most timeless and universal theme in literature worldwide. Yet my longing and need to go back have become more crucial in recent years because of the ongoing political, cultural, and environmental struggles facing the Southwest. The area is in the news on a regular basis. NAFTA, the drug wars, immigration, and the popular literary genre of nature writing have placed west Texas and southern New Mexico in the spotlight. There is a great deal about their present and future to write about. Dozens of writers have been doing it because they notice it is a hotbed of concern and a stage for encounters between powerful forces. In the midst of this debate over the future state of the borderlands, and as a native, I record what once was. Hopefully I have done this in a sacred, though unsentimental, manner. I visit to mourn the past and encompass what is left untouched in the desert. I return to get my bearings for writing about its future.

Memory Fever is about growing up in a place I will not see again. My first twenty-seven years in El Paso were a time of wonder, of waking to the mysteries of the desert, and a period of familial and cultural conflict. This book is not so much an autobiography as it is a record of childhood, youth, and departure. These essays were written over a period of years and often arose from ideas for failed poems. This is an odd thing to admit because a poet's failed work usually remains in a notebook or on a forgotten floppy disc. When the poet does open old work that he has been struggling with, there is a chance that some of the writing will become successful poetry. These essays were seeded in fragments for poems but turned into prose because I could not tell these stories in poetic language. When the book was first published in 1993, I was drawn to my favorite ones when I recognized the hidden poems in each. Six years later, I see this collection as a true text of memory—an attempt to recall my early years in a unique part of the country and the struggle to recreate the emotional break with my home. Readers familiar with my writing can say I have been doing exactly these things in my poetry, but I would disagree. After years of writing, I believe the pure language of memory is the essay. Given the wider canvas of nonfiction, I found more to write about because historical, autobiographical, and cultural events in El Paso kept revealing themselves in periods of detailed revelation. On the other hand, the language of visionary enactment, which borrows from memory and imagination, is the poem. Also, the fact I have always written about such a complex area as the U.S.–Mexican border calls for a varied approach to what I want to say about my life there. This book is a companion to my volumes of poetry and extends my desire to know my past the way I know it in my poems. Like those individual poems with their specific moments, these essays stand alone. Like any complete book of poetry, they also weave together to extend the voice of the writer until the private life becomes a universal call for understanding and redemption.

Childhood is a common topic for many writers. It can be the easiest thing to write about if you wish to describe common behavior, like playing with toys, being taken care of, or going to school for the first time. My childhood recollections are drawn from the realization that I spent many of those years alone and had to turn to the natural world for solace. As a child, I had to deal with parental absence and maternal myths—dark forces that influenced one's self-confidence, artistic development, and the need to find solitude in an overwhelming natural environment. These visions of my early years in El Paso are also portraits of growing up in a time of innocence, where the concept of an ideal family structure and the magical wonders of a beautiful terrain had not yet been shattered. The essays on high school, music, and the self-discovery that led to writing are memories that laid the foundation for what I would write later in life and what I am still attempting to do. My childhood memories are about a family that gave me the gift of creativity. Amidst the pain and the joy, it is a book for them.

I find the short, imagistic essay the most effective tool in painting this world of the Rio Grande and the Chihuahuan Desert. It serves my purposes in dealing with parental disintegration and documenting the clash between border cultures. In the essay "The Grandeur of the Grand Canyon" Diane Ackerman writes, "In a world governed by proportion—in which the eye frames a moment, digests it, frames another—scale is lost; visual scale, mental scale, emotional scale." *Memory Fever* is about recapturing these scales of the Southwest by finding the path of my youth within it while celebrating the grand power of its natural world before encroachment.

This difficult book to write is filled with awe and acts of learning and doing. It is my first tribute to my home, but it will not be the last. The title essay is a transition piece toward distance, wisdom, and the future. Forthcoming essays will deal with the environmental and cultural realities of life on the border as the new century arrives. In *Walden* there is a popular quote from Henry Thoreau in which he says, "By a conscious effort of the mind, we can stand aloof from actions and their consequences." He was writing about the power of nature and how he found sanctuary from human behavior by forming a relationship with the earth. My essays are not about polarity or creating new borders between the frailty of people and the vulnerability of the desert terrain. They are about taking the consequences of our daily lives and finding new hope as we wander across a precious landscape we were fortunate to have been given.

I would like to thank John Ellison and Leslie Link of Broken Moon Press, who believed in this book and originally published it in 1993. My gratitude is extended to Patti Hartmann at the University of Arizona Press for her continuing support of my work. Friends and family in El Paso, Denver, San Antonio, Chicago, and Minneapolis have been tremendous boosters over the years. Special recognition goes to the University of Minnesota for a McKnight Land Grant Professorship, a major fellowship that has given me time to return to the Southwest to rediscover this book and to research future ones.

BEGINNINGS

Mi Tierra

We understand what we need and throw our lives into the Sonora and Chihuahua deserts, boundaries for the dust where the family lived and died, where we grew up, the ghosts of *conquistadores* marching and dictating our view of life and death in the desert, the conquest making us wonder what happened to the pueblo people. Where are the skeletons of the Spanish soldiers buried? Where did they dissolve into the earth? In what year did our first *mestizo* great-grandparents cross the Rio Grande?

It is the story that survives dust storms and little rain. Tales of life, death, and wonder in a desert of deceptive beauty—the place where the earth accepted its fate at the hands of the pueblo people who fought to save their civilization, and of the Spanish explorers who came to cut open the earth for its riches and to burn the pueblos down. The Spanish did not know it would never be enough. Their journey north would influence the location of *El Paso del Norte,* the desolate settlement around the constantly changing course of the river. Rio Grande—its many names deceiving those who tried to cross it and take what they wanted—Rio Grande, Rio de las Palmas, Rio de San Buenaventura del Norte, Rio de Nuestra Señora, Rio de la Conception.

It is a simple truth—we no longer cross the Rio Grande in vain as the conquistadores did. When we cross the muddy river, it is for family reasons. We are branded illegals no

matter which side of the border we come from. There are
too many old desires to be satisfied under the New Mexico
and west Texas sun. The ancient bones of these yearnings
roll in the wind, never dissolve, but drift over the desert in
the endless search for the vast, hot terrain of the adobe
home. "Tierra del Sol"—our refusal to die in the desert as
so many died before we were born in El Paso del Norte.

Who will believe us when we give up a few of our secrets? Who will rise to acknowledge that we are telling the
truth? Who will come out of their crumbling adobe houses
to greet the wandering man in the dirty robes, the stranger
who comes praying and calling across the *arroyos* and miles
of mesquite, the man who carries something in his folded
hands?

We want to understand what we dream, but we continue
to dream without understanding, exposing our hearts to the
dust where we sleep. Despite the hot ground, the earth
turns to give us a chance. It is a difficult vision having something to do with the recurring dream of the rattlesnake, the
creature of the desert that speaks in silence and waits for
the whole story to be told before darting or slithering toward the next boulder. It disappears, before crawling into
someone else's haunted dreams.

We cross the river without the snake because we want
to turn into stone monuments, to be discovered by the first
explorers who find the path to old adobe walls, artifacts
standing for centuries in the sun, refusing to topple in the
heat. The people of the desert *believe* in the adobe walls
and touch them once a day. The coolness of the hard mud
takes turns with the shimmering heat of the roof in protect-
ing anyone who hides within. People stand by these walls,
waiting for the stranger to come to their pueblo so they can
offer him gifts to carry in his cupped hands.

As the stranger approaches the pueblos, they ask the wind to explain what the families are doing in their houses. It is a quiet gathering, a wounding of old solitude and isolation you carry in your chest if you have been born and raised in the desert; a crossroads touching of various kinds, dark eyes and wisdom clashing under the clouds. Thousands of pueblo people are born hundreds of miles apart, broken treaties with each other now forgotten, new chants grabbing their tongues to protect them against the approaching stranger.

Suddenly you recognize him as the saint maker—the silent one who goes from pueblo to pueblo carving wooden statues of saints, teaching the skeptical how to make *retablos,* tablets containing the colorful etchings and lifelike images of the saints who hide in the desert hills and who warn those who approach as the saint maker brings his crafts to the next pueblo. In his pack, he even carries *bultos*—doll-like figures he carved to remind us that our dead family members will never disappear. They are carved into these dolls and hidden among the holy statues—an act some frown upon as going against the desert god, but the carvings of our dead grandparents survive among the blessed because the saint maker is one of the first and oldest men to welcome you into the desert, one of the first you dream about when you realize, as a child, that you are growing up in a land where too many things have happened, that too many secrets lie buried in the sand.

As he enters the pueblo, the saint maker is welcomed because he participates in your story. He lets the people form a circle around his possessions, your mother and grandmother looking through the bultos, hoping to recognize a face and body that means they no longer have to grieve. The saint maker allows them to unveil the loaf of bread they carry with care to place in his bowl, and they warn him never to look down at the falling crumbs because they will fall through his outstretched hands.

The Light

Fernando runs down the street looking for the light his brothers told him was running ahead of him. They tell him every night, and he takes off, running down the street like a *vato loco*, searching for the bright ball that his brothers claim waits for him on every street corner, waits for him to catch up and appreciate what the light can do for him. He takes off down the dark streets of the barrio, but he is not afraid of trouble from strange *vatos* hiding behind the parked cars. He is afraid of not finding the light his brothers claim is there. They all say they have seen it at night. They laugh when Fernando tells them he has not seen it.

Roberto with the scar on his face and the cool shades says he has seen it more than anyone else. He describes the light better than any of the brothers. As he listens, Fernando wonders what Roberto is talking about and questions whether he has really seen it. Then Fernando realizes that he may be different from the other brothers; he wonders if he will ever see it, if he can run fast enough to catch up with the light.

They say it is right on the corner of Durazno and Piedras Streets, never in front of Chata's liquor store. Fernando tries to catch his breath as he reaches the corner, but he does not see the light. It is late evening and he would know if it was there. The street lamp on the telephone pole is broken and missing a light; the liquor store is closed.

Fernando knows he must find the light tonight, or he can't go back to the vatos like he is one of them. Suddenly he sees something flickering down the street, and he takes off. It bounces off the windshields of the parked cars, its radiance is waiting for him in the middle of the street. The sweat runs down his face as he reaches the next corner.

He gasps and coughs, but smiles because the light is there! The light he has been chasing through the barrio is finally waiting for him. He is going to catch up to take a good look at it. He pants and walks the last few yards and stops in front of a short vato, a brother walking coolly down the street. Fernando looks at him and sees a light radiating from his body.

"*Esé*," he calls to the vato whose face he can hardly make out in the strange combination of dark and light. The bright haze that hangs over both of them does not help him identify the vato. The boy turns without a word, and Fernando notices he looks like Victor, a brother who died in a gang fight seven years ago.

Fernando is not sure this is Victor. He is not frightened as he stops walking alongside the light and the boy. He watches the boy cross the road toward the old freeway, making the black houses of the barrio shine with a brightness that the vatos know is there and can never burn out.

PART ONE

The Sparrows

The memory of dead sparrows arises from the desire to be there, again, on the July afternoon when the rainstorm came close to being a hurricane in the desert. It rolled through a black sky, a rumbling wall of water crossing from Mexico to hit El Paso with seven inches of rain in less than two hours. It crashed into the cottonwoods in front of my house, tearing the green branches off in a splintering roar of water, wind, and raindrops like steel pellets.

Hundreds of sparrows made nests in those trees every evening. They would land in clusters and fill the branches with constant chirping. The gray cottonwoods were brown with the thick mass of birds that occupied the trees.

The mystery I had witnessed several times and found fascinating was the way the birds stopped chirping all at once! This happened every evening as I stood on the porch while the sun burned orange in the western sky over the Rio Grande. The birds would suddenly be quiet, at once, on a single note. One second, the loud chirping would drown other noises in the area. The next, they would stop together, as if on cue. The unexpected silence forcefully swept through the trees. Then they would resume chirping, hundreds of them together.

I had witnessed this silence just a few minutes before the storm from Mexico washed violently across the river, smashing against the house. The house shook in the downpour, the weight of the rain breaking the trees, carrying branches and chunks of earth in rushing streams that flooded the yard and threatened the house. I stood on the porch as rain pounded the roof. The shrieking wind threw water in all directions. I was soaked despite the shelter of the porch. I didn't want to go into the house—I had never seen a storm like this one.

The afternoon turned into a deep purple night. The sky was a black and purple mass, the colors growing deeper as the storm moved north in a deafening rush. Bushes and the trees in the yard bent low to the ground, their leaves shot off by giant raindrops. A sea of mud, grass, and leaves rose suddenly, and then a loud crack echoed across the sky and lightning flashed. Dozens of dead sparrows were floating everywhere.

During most rainstorms, birds taking shelter in the trees survive. This time, the rain was too overwhelming and powerful. Unable to fly, they were swept off the trees with the leaves and branches, washed and scattered over the area that turned into a small lake. The water rose as the black fist of the storm passed. The porch flooded; I stood ankle deep in rising mud. Another flash of lightning finally drove me inside. I was wet, with no time to change because water was coming into the house. The sight of all those dead sparrows stayed in my mind as I frantically moved furniture and books to high and dry places in the house.

By the next morning, all the rooms were flooded. Six inches of mud covered the floors. I worked all day to clean the mess. The sun shone brightly in a clear, blue sky. The yard and streets were one huge, muddy lake. As I spent the day cleaning, a foul smell hung over the area. The canal behind the house had overflowed, its green slime eroding much of the bank around the cement channel.

In the afternoon, I went outside to get away from cleaning. Dead birds littered the yard, brown and yellow sparrows that looked like stuffed toy birds. Bloated bodies floated delicately among uprooted trees and crushed bushes, the water not moving anywhere, the lake containing whole flocks of drowned birds. This was the source of the stench, as the sun steamed over the devastated yard.

I counted over two hundred birds near the porch and estimated another three hundred spread throughout the yard. I waited one more day for the water to recede and the yard to start drying. When I was able to walk in the mud two days after the storm, the smell was unbearable. I knew what I had to do.

I buried over eight hundred sparrows in a huge *arroyo* carved out of the yard by the rushing water. I gathered them in shovelfuls all day long. By evening, I had cleared much of the yard, but I knew I could not find every dead bird in the mess. Many would simply dissolve into the ground. I piled the tiny bodies in the arroyo, filled it with mud, covered and leveled it.

Walking back to the house, I noticed the familiar sound for the first time since the storm. The bare branches of the tree were full of sparrows, more birds than ever before. They had returned to fill the air with singing. I stood on the porch, listened to the chirping, and waited until they quieted at once, all on one note. I went into the house when they started singing together, again.

The Burning

Light flashed across the summer night. It was brilliant—a blue and white streak falling over the dark sandhills to hit the earth without a sound. The hot June night returned to its black beauty, thousands of stars glittering above the desert. The plain of the sky extended its arms over the horizon, trying to cover the endless terrain of desert with stars constantly moving to keep up with the vastness. I was near Kilbourne Hole, an extinct volcano fifty miles due west of El Paso, its rim eroded flat, its bottom reaching toward the surface after millions of years of thrusting against the evolving sands. Any vehicle attempting to reach the crater must bounce over miles of dirt roads to get to the volcano few people know exists.

The sudden light scared me out of my quiet vigil by my small campfire. I jumped up with the impulse to bolt into my Jeep and leave, afraid that something was going to fall on me. But what was the flash I had seen? My first wild thought was that a meteor had crashed, but that was highly unlikely. In the black desert night, away from the glow of the city lights, it was easy to spot falling stars streaking across the sky. I had already counted eight in an hour. It's a sight hard to catch in the city.

But I hesitated. I wondered if an object would crash nearby. The petrifying stillness of the desert made me shiver. I moved closer to the rim of the volcano, but it was pitch black across its diameter. After millions of years of

erosion, the volcano was only fifty feet deep. Its crater of
lava cliffs and black rocks rose in odd shapes, about a mile
across. In the darkness, beyond the petrified volcano walls,
the glow where the bright object had fallen silhouetted the
top of the sand dunes and mesquite bushes that lined the
volcano's rim. I kicked dirt on the dying fire and climbed
into my Jeep.

Before turning on the headlights, I sat and waited—in
complete darkness. The glow grew brighter. I estimated it
to be four or five miles away. I could probably reach it by
driving around Kilbourne Hole, but the sudden, falling light
made me hesitate. Was it a UFO? I hadn't heard an explosion or felt an impact. I had never seen UFOs in the desert.

I started the engine and drove the Jeep across the narrow dirt road that was the only access to the volcano. It was
barely wide enough for one vehicle, having been cut into
the thick, sandy area covered with black rocks and deep
holes. The Jeep bounced over the hard surface, the thick
mesquite branches scratching its sides loudly as the Jeep
squeezed through thick clusters of full-grown barrel cactus,
Spanish daggers, and salt cedars. Several kangaroo rats and
jack rabbits bounced in the beam of the headlights and then
disappeared. I hit a large rock as I swerved around a curve
in the road. The Jeep bounced and came down with a crash.
I slowed to five miles an hour, downshifted, and made another turn. I braked in front of a barbed-wire gate and got
out, unlatched it, and drove through. Stopping to close the
gate behind me, I looked north to see the glow increase in
intensity.

I drove for another mile until I found the side road I
had been looking for. It turned east toward Kilbourne Hole
for a couple of hundred yards, and then twisted north. I followed it slowly, sections of it almost impassable with rocks

and dead mesquite. I finally hit a large rise and skidded over the top. I pulled around a ridge and turned off the head-lights.

The desert was on fire! An area about a hundred yards wide and twice as long was burning. Mesquite bushes were ablaze like hundreds of campfires. The sweet smell of scorched green wood rose in a haze, covering the clear night sky. I looked for a crater or clue as to what had fallen. This had to be the result of the streak of light I saw, but again, I had not heard an explosion. The earth was undis-turbed. There was no sign of an impact.

I started down the ridge. Loose gravel and rocks rolled to the bottom. Mesquite smoldered and popped, already burned down to tiny, black stumps. Each bush grew a few yards from the next without forming a wooded floor; this fire was not likely to spread very far.

I stared at a sight I had never witnessed before. Moving carefully through the maze of fires, I searched for the source. I waved my flashlight in all directions (even though the flames made it unnecessary). Closer inspection con-firmed what I had seen from the ridge—smooth ground and burning mesquite, as if someone had take a flame-thrower and swept it over the low vegetation.

My eyes watered from the smoke. I turned to climb up the ridge and I felt something flick against my arms and legs. Dozens of grasshoppers were jumping into the nearest flames. They were everywhere. The fire must have brought them out. It was the same magnetic attraction that a moth has to a light bulb—pure sacrifice. In the desert night, the grasshoppers came out in mass to hurtle themselves into the hissing mesquite.

Within minutes, the fires died down and smoldered, dimming into a low bed of embers and charred sticks. I scanned the area one last time with the flashlight but did not see anything. I paused on the ridge top and looked down with watering eyes. The crackling of the mesquite and grasshoppers ceased quickly. I rested against the hood of the Jeep and looked up at the sky. I started to turn the flashlight off when I spotted something else near my boot— a large, black tarantula hurrying across the dirt. It vanished under a rock.

I wanted to see another shooting star, so it could tell me what this fire was all about. What had dropped here? Who would believe I saw this? It never took long to spot a falling star in the desert. I sat on the hood and waited, hoping something would reveal itself as the source of the burning. The smoke and smell of the mesquite blended into a scent that covered me and slowly eased my concern about the mysterious fire. I stared up at the Big Dipper, squinted through the smoke and tried to identify other constellations. I anticipated the next falling star, so I waited. Minutes passed. The desert was no longer burning. A field of embers radiated over the area. It was unusual not to see a falling star by now.

I would never discover what ignited the mesquite and hypnotized the grasshoppers. I would not spot any more falling stars that night. I climbed into the Jeep, gave one last look at the constant sky, and drove slowly away, a fire of solitude smoldering in my pounding heart.

Rattlesnake Dreams

have dreamed about rattle-
snakes for many years, which has resulted in a sequence of
poems written over those same years. I do not know why I
dream about snakes or why I am fascinated by rattlers,
those powerful, elusive creatures few people see in the desert. They are out there, even though their habitat has been
reduced by suburban growth. As time and civilization pass
through the deserts of the Southwest, fewer humans will
encounter them, except in zoos or movies.

How many people who live in New Mexico, Arizona, or
west Texas have recurring dreams about diamond-back
rattlesnakes? Do the dreams have to do with growing up in
the desert and having killed rattlesnakes as a boy? Do my
dreams and snake poems have to do with the myths of my
ancestors, who came from northern Mexico and settled in
the Sonora desert of Arizona, their houses and working
environment surrounded by those elusive, unpredictable
reptiles?

Rattlesnake Dream

I thought the rattlesnake was dead
and I stuck my finger in its mouth,
felt the fangs bite down,
penetrate me without letting go,
the fire removing my eyes,
replacing them with green light
of the reptile that illuminated my hand.

It entered my bone and blood,
until my whole arm was green and damp,
my whole left side turning
slick and cool as
I tried to pull it
out of my body.

I peeled my skin back
to find my veins were green
and held tightly what I believed,
what forced itself into me,
what I allowed to be given
without knowing

I would carry that secret,
crawl over the ground,
become a fusion of muscle
only the sun steps on.
I leaned against a huge boulder,
sweated, waited, slept,
and, by morning, found a new way
of embracing that rock,
new life in the green flesh
of the world.

This was the first snake dream in which I touched a
snake. In earlier dreams, I walk across the desert and the
Rio Grande River. The ground is seething with snakes, dozens of them coming out of the earth, but none bite or
threaten me. I walk through the twisting, moving shapes
without fear. This new version of my reptilian journey
marks the first time I approached a snake to touch it.

I am standing in someone's front yard. There is an old
adobe house a few yards away. A giant cottonwood tree with
its huge trunk and limbs parts above my head. A dark-
skinned man stands by the tree, holding a rattlesnake in his

hands. I do not know him. I cannot see his face clearly. He holds the snake like an experienced snake handler. I walk up to him and see that the snake is dead. He cradles it in his arms without fear. I reach out and run my fingers over the cool, slick head of the rattler. Its eyes are closed.

I carefully move a finger to the tip of its head, and then quickly stick my finger inside its mouth. I am not afraid. I know the mouth of the dead rattler will open for me, and it does. I push my finger deeper to feel the fangs.

Suddenly the snake comes to life and clamps down hard on my finger. But I do not scream or jump back; the snake handler does not pull the snake away. I feel a strange kind of contentment. The snake will not let go. I am not surprised. The man disappears. The snake dangles in the air, hooked onto my hand.

The dream shifts, and changes pace and scene. I am walking along the river. It is near nightfall. I wander somewhere in La Mesilla Valley, north of El Paso. The snake has entered my body through my hand and fist. It has become my arm. As I walk, I peel back the shedding skin on my left hand to expose the bright green veins and muscles of my flesh. The snake has traveled up my bones and blood to become a part of me. I keep walking along the river. My whole body is damp and cool, as if I had crawled out of the river, out of a dark place. I feel no pain, do not suffer, do not panic. This is not a nightmare. It is a trance of motion; I hear low rattling and have the sense that more snakes are about to crawl out of the ground at my feet. I keep walking along the river.

Then I wake up.

It is a peaceful awakening, but I cannot get the dream out of my mind. I think about it for several days and then write the poem. The questions return. I go through my notebooks to read earlier snake poems, trying to find a clue as to why I absorbed this snake when my earlier dreams were passive. Were my questions about rattlesnakes being answered? Did this dream take me back to my childhood, when I first encountered baby rattlesnakes? When I killed several of them, once in our neighbor's front yard, and one in a crucial encounter behind my house?

Several of my snake poems are about these killings, the only times I chanced getting bitten as a kid who played and wandered in the desert for many years. I was twelve years old when our neighbor Martha came to our door and told me there were three or four baby rattlers in her flower box. Her sons and husband were not home. She was afraid the snakes were going to get into the house or bite someone. She asked if I would take the shovel that she held in her hands and kill them for her. She thrust the long wooden handle of the shovel at me. Hesitant, I stood in the doorway.

I don't recall if my mother was home, or who else was around, but I took the shovel and carefully walked back to Martha's house with her. I had seen a few snakes in the desert hills across the street and heard a few rattles in the tumbleweeds, but I had never tried to kill or confront any of them.

I spotted three snakes curled around each other under one of Martha's rose bushes. They looked like thick pieces of string, each one not more than ten inches long. The baby rattlers were a pale, fleshy color with their heads almost invisible. They had not developed their rattles yet. I could see the rattle's nub at the end of their bodies.

I stood about six feet away and did not move for several seconds. I was not really afraid, but what would a twelve-year-old with a big shovel do at a moment like this? Charge and chop everything to pieces? I stood there with Martha saying, "Go on, kill them!" She backed off and waited for me to do something. The snakes moved and continued to wrap themselves around each other, becoming a single creature.

"Go on, kill them!"

I turned to look at Martha and noticed how quiet the neighborhood was in the middle of the afternoon. How did she know that I didn't go to school that day? I saw one of the snakes separate itself from the other two and I stepped forward, using the shovel as a spear. Without aiming or pausing, I lanced the snake behind the head and watched it come apart. The two pieces split into the ground. The other snakes reacted by separating from each other. I hacked at the second one. The shovel pushed the head into the dirt. The third snake disappeared under another bush. I moved back a few feet, watching the writhing, dying snakes. I expected lots of blood but did not see any. The baby rattlers soon stopped squirming.

"How many did you kill?" Martha asked me, her hands covering her mouth. She could clearly see I had gotten two. We couldn't find the third one.

I turned to her but didn't say a word. I still recall staring at her in silence. I did not know what to say as I handed her the shovel. She took it and watched me leave, the expression on my face preventing her from saying anything else to me. I cannot recall what else happened that day. That was more than twenty-six years ago. Killing the two snakes contributes to my not remembering the rest of the day, how I was able to kill the snakes with a rare bravery, a recklessness that could have gotten me bitten.

My second encounter with snakes may be the crucial doorway into my dreams. A couple of summers later, my mother saw four baby rattlers in our backyard. She closed the sliding doors leading to the porch and told me not to go out. She panicked and wanted to call pest control. I knew it was up to me, and I was less hesitant this time.

I used a shovel again. This time, I was more careful and noticed that the four snakes looked similar to the ones at Martha's house. I hacked at one, cutting it into pieces. I killed two more with one swing and loud thud of the shovel. Their bodies remained knotted together, their entrails streaking across the metal head of the shovel, one of the tiny snakes opening its jaws at me as it came apart in the grass. With my heart racing and sweat running down my forehead onto my eyeglasses, I looked wildly for the fourth rattler. Through the wet, distorted vision of my lenses, I saw the snake crawl up the bricks of the house to disappear into a crack in the overhanging roof. Before I knew it, it vanished into the wall of the house. My mother was going to be horrified.

I stood there and stared at the dead snakes. I couldn't take my eyes off the head of the one that died with its miniature white fangs bared to the sun and pointed at me, the jaws wide open as if to swallow my bravery completely. I could see the beautiful diamond patterns starting to develop on its torn skin. I did not want to tell my mother one of the snakes slithered into the wall. My failure was not so much in losing a snake, but in the fact that its turning toward my mother's place of safety would create resentment on her part. This only added to my shame, my sense of failure about confronting these mysterious creatures.

I dug a hole near a dry spot in the flower box and shoveled the dead snakes into it. The sweat ran down my glasses, so I couldn't see clearly what was left of the snakes. I did not stop to wipe my glasses until I covered the hole with dirt and packed it down. I wanted this mutilation to disappear into the safe ground.

When I told her what happened, my mother called pest control. The man came out and said the snake would die inside the walls. He didn't think it could actually come into the house. My mother worried for several days. I remember her asking me in an anguished voice, "Why didn't you kill them all? What are we going to do with a snake loose in the house?"

Without realizing it at the time, I was consumed with guilt. I had done something terribly wrong by letting the snake get into the wall. What was a fourteen-year-old supposed to do? I was good with the shovel, but what was I doing killing snakes for other people and not completing the job, letting two of them get away?

I have never forgotten the snake that rushed up the bricks to escape my attack. It could be the seed planted for my recurring dreams. Part six of my poem "Rattlesnake Dance, Coronado Hills, 1966" reads:

> After killing three of them
> I saw the fourth one climb up the porch,
> squeeze into the bricks and disappear
> into a corner of the house, its sleek body
> vanishing into the wall,
> becoming a part of our home.
>
> I never saw it, again,
> but lay awake at night,
> knowing it was inside the house,
> trapped between wood and mortar,
> moving from room to room without rattling,
> waiting for the walls to crumble in years,
> waiting for the boy to press his hands
> against the wall above his bed,
> and push in the dark,
> tap and push,

the silence of life
a falling black wall
that smothered every breath I took
as I waited and waited.

When I dream about snakes, there is a house nearby. I never go inside, but know it is my childhood home. It is the house the snake entered—to leave something with me— the snake I did not kill because it was quick and fast. Instinct told it where to go. Instinct saved it—and instinct shapes my snake dreams.

In his book *Symbols of Transformation,* Carl Jung writes about snakes coming from the world of instinct, involved with the vital processes of life that are not always apparent to us. He feels snake dreams personify hidden conflicts within us. An appearance by a green snake in a dream could mean danger.

In my early dreams, there is no sense of danger, only the house somewhere in the scene. The ground is covered with snakes, hundreds of them moving between my legs as I walk peacefully along the river on a bright, sunny day. The snakes keep coming out of the ground. In one dream, they come out of a freshly dug pit. Where is my shovel?

Suddenly I am in the most recent dream. The veins and muscles in my left arm have turned green. In other dreams, I cannot identify the colors of the rattlers—there are so many snakes, the darkness of their numbers makes it impossible to recall colors. The one time I can identify a color, it becomes the green snake of danger and has entered my body.

What danger is this? As I try to relive those incidents of killing the baby rattlers, I know I overcame my fear. The harder thing to bring back is the guilt and sense of failure that I did not kill every snake that was threatening those women and the tranquillity of their homes. The ones that got away inhabit my dreams. If there is a danger, it is the fact that I have been stuck in the cycle of wandering over ground covered with snakes—the desert of my lonely childhood experiences as an only son.

This sets off the recurring dreams and the snake poems that tell me that I did not finish my job as the snake killer. I sleep and go back to the snakes, but I do not kill them. I do not lift shovels and tear baby rattlers apart. The snakes are alive to be a part of my dreams, even the one that pretends it is dead, so that I can come to it. The green snake that is becoming my arm is consuming me in order to force me to complete the cycle and get the job done. But I do not dream killing dreams. Death is not a part of the fertile ground covered with thick, diamond-back rattlesnakes.

Of course, I will not go out and find a real snake, kill it, and rid myself of the baby rattlers that became grown snakes in my dreams. Instead, I complete the cycle by writing poems, allowing myself to go back to the killings I carried out for the women. I must accept the fact that I did what I could, and let the river of living snakes flow in my dreams.

What about the green snake in my body? It is the snake that entered my house through the wall. I hacked those rattlers with a strong swing of my left arm. I am right-handed.

My conscious mind says that I was told to kill the snakes by two women who were frightened, though they must have known that snakes are a hazard of living in the desert. I cut the snakes without much hesitation. Who could ask more from a teenaged boy who had never killed snakes before? For several weeks, my mother could not get over the fact that there was a snake in the walls. I lay awake at night, listening through the walls of my bedroom to see if I could hear the rattle, find out if the snake was going to get its revenge against the young killer. Instinct tells me that I became the snake that got away. It becomes my being by traveling through my body, reaching my heart, letting me open the earth to allow new-born rattlers to emerge into the light.

If the green snake brings any other signs of danger, they point to my family and our personal history. Killing the snakes for my mother meant I was a good boy defending my home. Letting one of them enter the house meant that I was not quite what she expected me to be. My mother eventually forgot the snake incident and life went on. I do not recall seeing snakes in our yard again. As a matter of fact, it was the last time I saw any rattlers in my twenty-five years of living in El Paso.

I started having snake dreams after I left El Paso and moved to Denver. I was gone from the desert and lived a different life. The dreams began. Distance and time, and my intense separation from the desert triggered the release of those snakes. The dreams happen three or four times a year. They never come as nightmares. I wake in a peaceful state and never see the dreams as signs of danger. If Jung is correct, the dreams are speaking of an unsettled killing, a flawed act of bravery, an incomplete hunt before the matriarchal audience, a family history shaped in the desert to turn out in ways I could not foresee.

The Navajo believe snake dreams are not serious or threatening, unless you are bitten in the dream. When I stuck my finger into the snake's mouth, I did not feel a real bite, even though the snake took hold of me. It was a feeling of pressure, a slow evolution up my arm, a sudden, energetic flowing—an awakening within my reptilian sleep. Was it a bite? According to Navajo belief, this is the most

serious dream, the one that led me to ponder this as I continue writing my snake poems.

> I leave after searching each stall,
> but the boa and copperhead have a long way
> to go before turning blue, neither one
> knowing me when I killed blue lightning
> to prevent a storm of open flesh,
> drove metal through muscled ground
> in search of blood that never came,
> my wonder over the clean pieces
> sending the snake on its way
> before I could enter the glass,
> find the hidden blue eyes sparkling
> off the wire where the rattle
> misses a beat for me.
>
> (from "The Blue Snake")

I remember the color blue when I think of the baby rattlers, never the color green from my later dream. Baby
rattlers have a pale sheen. I see their quick bodies in flashes
of blue. "The Blue Snake" refers to a dream in which I find
myself in a zoo reptile house, searching for the snakes
I killed and the ones that got away.

A couple of years ago, after one of the dreams in which I
walked in a swampy area near the river, the ground covered
with harmless rattlesnakes, I woke and lay quietly in the
dark. I thought back to killing the baby rattlers. I could still
feel the sensation of snakes crawling between my legs without harming me, dozens of them sliding in and out of the
river. I was not afraid, and I lay there knowing that I had
not felt threatened at the age of twelve when I first killed
the snakes. I was simply doing a favor for someone. The
later killings helped a more immediate person and involved

my house. After several of these dreams, I admitted that I
was fascinated by the surviving snake crawling into the
wall. I was curious as to how a snake could survive or die inside the walls. That was more important than pleasing my
mother. As I lay in my bed, breathing after the latest dream,
I could finally admit it to myself.

The dream of walking along the river occurred earlier
than the most recent one in which the snake becomes my
arm. The first dream took my fear away. The second dream
made me reach out to the snakes for the first time. It was a
cycle in completion, closing upon the circle like a snake de-
vouring its own body, consuming my arm to settle within
me in a startling, non-threatening way.

I accept the dream about the green snake as a sign that
the baby rattler that got away grew beyond the walls of the
house to be spared by fate and the actions of a boy responding to command. I had to spare the snakes. As I relive the
images of hacking at them with the shovel, I know the baby
rattlers were fast but I could have killed them all. As I
dream, I let some of them go—I have an inner need to not
kill everything threatening the neighborhood, my mother,
our house!

Native American people have a general taboo against
killing snakes. Tuscarora Indians are afraid to kill rattlers
out of fear that the snake's relatives will return to seek revenge. The Tarahumara Indians of Mexico believe that the
rattlers are companions of sorcerers, who meet and talk
with them. Meskwaki Indians believe in the rattlesnake as
an instrument of punishment. The Chiricahua Apaches of
Arizona have a dread of rattlers that goes beyond the fear
of snake bite. They address rattlesnakes as "mother's mother," and have a restriction among their people against talking about snakes. I find this amazing for a tribe of the

Sonora desert, one of the richest habitats of giant diamond-back rattlers, the most poisonous of the twenty-five species of rattlesnakes in the U.S.

The only other time I came close to confronting a rattlesnake was in 1986, on a hike with my poet-mentor Robert Burlingame. I was visiting my family in El Paso. Whenever I could, I would look up the wise, old poet and we would take long walks in the Franklin Mountains. We were climbing back down a narrow canyon on the eastern face of the Franklins after resting at the top.

He was walking in front of me and turned the corner around a huge boulder that lay in the narrow trail to the bottom. The rocks and dirt our feet rolled down warned the huge diamond-back sunning itself ten yards from Robert. We stopped immediately as the powerful rattle echoed against the steep, red walls of the canyon. We froze for a second, and then he pointed to it.

I could not see the snake clearly because it lay under a mesquite bush, but I could make out the thick roll as it slowly coiled back, ready to strike. Robert said quietly, "It's one of the biggest I have ever seen." I didn't say anything. Without hurry or panic, we stepped back and went around the snake from several yards away. We hopped over rough mesquite and Spanish dagger cactus, then moved back onto the smooth trail cut in the avalanche of rocks. I could hear the rattle as we left the snake behind, but I did not think about the snake dreams I had already had. I was too immersed in the pleasure of good company, hiking through the desert I loved, wondering why I didn't visit often enough; I did not think about the snake until later when the canyon encounter would result in my first snake poem, a piece I never knew would be the start of a long sequence of poems.

Diamond-Back on the Trail

We were climbing
down the canyon
when the sudden head
and rattle moved in the sun.

We froze in awe and respect
as it turned to us,
the enormous, poised body
revealing its claim
to the desert, its reason
for waking to challenge us,
to let us stand suspended
among the cactus and red rocks.

We stepped back as you said
it was one of the biggest
rattlers you had ever seen,
your years in the canyons
flashing in memory
like the snake's quick tongue
flicking at the crossing of time
and the way we all meet,
darting at the breathless way
we stumble upon the slithering heart,
the cold, slow muscle,
and the way we listen
to the loud rattling,
its blood in beauty one beat,
its bone and body
one movement into rock,
one sudden grasp at the earth.

Years and dreams later, the sudden grasp becomes the
boy walking along the river, then my finger in the snake's
mouth, forming itself into my arm in a cool, slow dream—a

trance in which the house stands there, creatures hidden in the walls, its history of being constructed in the desert, the story of people entering their own walls, trying to find their way over the constantly moving ground.

My snake dreams may never go away. I don't know how long the snake poem sequence will be. I continue to learn more about rattlesnakes. I wonder if boys today, living in desert towns like El Paso, will encounter snakes the way I did. Now Southwest streets in the 1990s have nothing to do with the waiting desert and its inhabitants. The baby rattlers have gone underground, away from brick walls and suburbs. They rise near the river where there are no houses, no chance to mistake neighborhoods for the fresh ground of the desert, the fertile, hot soil where muscled bone rises to shake a beat for those who dream and wonder.

The Third Eye of the Lizard

I killed hundreds of lizards when I was a boy. I shot them with my BB gun because it was a favorite sport my friends and mine. Shooting lizards helped to relieve the monotony of living in a small desert town. In 1963 my parents' house was built in a newly developed part of northwest El Paso. It sat on the outskirts of town, right in the middle of the desert, which meant that we were surrounded by rattlesnakes and lizards, creatures uprooted from their natural habitat by the new housing developments.

The empty lots around the house were havens for tumbleweeds and dozens of lizards. After a summer rain, I would walk through the lots, kick the weeds out of the way and watch the small gray and white lizards scatter for cover. I carried my loaded BB gun into the desert because I had a fantasy of shooting a huge rattlesnake, something that never happened. I killed many lizards without shame or guilt because I saw them as a threat to my life there, plus it was an ideal way to play out the timeless drama between the hunter and prey, the dance that begins when men are still boys.

Killing lizards became as routine as stepping on ants or swatting flies. There were endless numbers of lizards in the desert and many wandered into our yard, sunned themselves on the sidewalk, or crawled up the brick walls of the house. The most common was the collar lizard, four or five

inches long, counting the tail. The creatures were lightning
quick, but made good targets. When the lizards paused,
they reared up on their hind legs and trembled.

It was the moment to shoot. To be effective, you needed
to be at least ten feet close. (BB guns are not very accurate.)
I often missed, the pellet springing dirt into the air as the
pale lizard leaped away. When I got lucky and hit one, it
would bounce into the air and land on its back, twitching, its
white belly exposed to the sun. Then it would lie still.

During that moment, at the age of eleven, I felt powerful knowing I was a successful hunter—the conqueror, the
proud killer, the triumphant American soldier, a favorite
fantasy of young boys who dreamed beyond their big box of
plastic toy soldiers. I grew up watching violent cartoons
long before anyone cared to make an issue about the carnage kids were exposed to on TV. With my friends, I played
"army" and owned a huge pile of toy guns. I even got a G.I.
Joe the first year they were made in the early sixties. Getting my father to buy me a Daisy BB rifle was the next logi-
cal step. I had earned it by having many exciting adventures
and fantasies as a neighborhood soldier, defending the long
row of new houses against the dangers of living in the desert. By exterminating so many lizards, I kept the neighborhood safe. Dangers were tamed with my BB gun.

One summer I decided to keep track of how many lizards I killed by collecting their tails in a large matchbox.
It had never occurred to me to count tails until the first
time I encountered lizards shedding them. I cornered a
small lizard in a cardboard box one day, and decided not to
shoot it. I wanted a live one to exhibit in a glass jar I sometimes carried with me. Unafraid, I reached down to grab
the tiny thing. As I touched the tail, it came off. I was so
shocked, I dropped it. The tail shook by itself as the lizard

ran out of the box. I had never seen a tail with a life of its own.

This reflexive self-dismemberment, or autotomy as it is called, is a widely-known phenomenon among scientists who study such things, but it is a real shocker the first time you discover it. I stopped hunting lizards for several days after that, thinking that some evil desert spirit was punishing me for killing so many. But my friends told me it was part of being a lizard—the tail came off naturally and the lizard would grow a new one. I got over my guilt and proceeded to grab the tails of any lizards I shot. The tails always fell off, to twitch in the matchbox. I don't recall how many I had in the box when it disappeared one day. My mother probably found it. She must have screamed at the decaying little tails and thrown them away.

For awhile, my friends and I wanted to see twitching tails more than dead lizards. Instead of using our BB guns, we started going after the lizards with sticks to cut the tails off. We fell for a lizard's natural defense. If the lizard is frightened enough, touching its body is enough to cause a detachment of the tail. The tail then wiggles strongly and attracts more attention than the lizard. The reptiles in my neighborhood must have realized it was better to leave their tails behind than to be blown away. Casualties went down when my friends and I stood around watching little tails shaking on the ground while the bare-assed lizard took off. We must have eventually caught on though; after the first summer of discovering detachable tails, we went back to shooting the lizards.

By the age of thirteen, after I discovered rock-and-roll music, I lost interest in guns and killing lizards forever. My last summer of killing them is memorable—my greatest challenge as a hunter came with the appearance of the biggest lizard I had ever seen in the neighborhood. This huge reptile so threatened my territory it made me carry extra BB pellets in the pockets of my torn Levi's.

I first saw it clinging to the back door that led into the garage. It was a fat, dark-brown lizard measuring a good ten inches. It was not a collar lizard. I first thought it was a Gila monster, but knew they didn't exist in Texas, only in the Sonora desert of Arizona. (I had looked that up in the school encyclopedia long ago.)

I grabbed my BB gun and fired the first shot from several yards away. I missed and heard the thunk of the pellet embedding itself in the wooden door. The huge lizard darted into a crevice between the roof of the house and the doorway. I was excited, but knew I should have gotten closer. Usually, I was a very patient hunter, and my friends always kidded me because I was the best marksman among us.

I saw it again a few days later. It lay along the edge of the concrete flower bed in the backyard. I stepped closer and fired from about six feet away. The shot ricocheted off the cement and the lizard flew off. I thought I hit it, but could find no trace of it in the flower box.

I did not see the mysterious, dark creature for over two weeks, until one day I walked past the garage door to find it near the same spot where it had first appeared. I aimed carefully and fired. I missed again and was stunned to see the lizard did not move or run. I quickly recocked the single-shot air rifle and fired a second time. The second pellet buried itself in the door with my other stray shots. The lizard fell with a thud and then ran under the door. It disappeared in a stack of firewood inside the garage.

I counted the BBs stuck in the door and couldn't believe the strange luck of this reptile. I went to the woodpile and kicked logs around until heard a scraping sound underneath. The lizard was trapped, but I couldn't see it. I came back the next day, poked around and heard it. I wondered why it didn't run out the door. Maybe lizards with their reptilian brains were still not smart enough to find their way out of a room. I waited in the garage, but it didn't come out.

For five days I went into the garage without flushing it out. On the morning of the sixth day, as I crossed the backyard toward the garage, I saw the lizard sitting high on the brick wall of the house. It had finally made its move. I cocked the rifle, aimed, and slowly drew closer. I fired from a few feet away.

The lizard flew off the wall and landed behind two trash cans. It shivered for a few seconds, its large brown feet outstretched, its long, thick tail twitching slowly. Watching it die, I was suddenly afraid. This was the biggest thing I had killed. I felt panic and guilt I had never encountered before as a boy with a nasty BB gun. I was too shaken to bury the lizard or throw it into the trash can. I knew the ants would get it soon. (It was a common sight to walk through the desert and see red army ants picking clean the tiny skeletons of dead lizards.)

The day after I shot the big lizard, I came back to the trash cans to see what the ants had done. The lizard's thick body lay on its stomach. When I hit it, it had landed on its back. I wondered if ants had the power to turn it over.

Hundreds of them crawled over the body. They had eaten half of the right side around its belly. My shot had split its back, offering another entry for the carnivorous ants. What struck me that day was the sudden appearance of a rough, round band on top of the lizard's head. I bent over to study it closer. I had never seen such a design on a lizard. The circle on its head was a lighter brown, almost pale red, and looked like a marking you might find on a rattlesnake. As I gazed at the intricate colorings on the dead animal, the sense of dread and guilt returned. I walked away and did not check on the lizard for several days. When I came back, it was gone. The only trace was a dark spot of blood and the remains of a gnarled foot. Even the skeleton was gone.

Years later, I came across the key to the circle on the lizard's head. In his book *Desert Journal* (University of California, 1977), naturalist Raymond Cowles writes that some species of lizards have a third eye on top of their heads. He calls them parietal eyes and says researchers have found no mechanism for vision in the third eye. He feels the parietal eye in lizards helps regulate daily and seasonal exposure to sunlight, but there are theories some dinosaurs and ancient reptiles may have had a third eye once, a good extra eyeball for defense against approaching enemies.

In his essay "The Three Brains," poet Robert Bly speculates about which parts of ourselves have not truly evolved, and which parts of our brains remain reptilian. He speculates that we all have reptilian brains working to think about the need for food, survival, and security. Perhaps this is what made the lizard so elusive and mysterious, an unexplainable connection to both of our reptilian states. Did the lizard dodge so many of my BBs because it was watching me the whole time? Did I kill lizards because I wanted to survive in the desert without hidden eyes witnessing everything I did? Later in the essay, Bly announces that the desert landscape rarely contains mammal images. He feels that lizards and snakes dominate and influence the way we behave when we live in such arid places.

The lizard I killed had a third eye, and my memory of it on its head is an image that is reptilian, not mammalian. The third eye closes around the mysteries of the desert and how living in it is crucial to learning why we hide ourselves in our three brains. Its third eye made sure I recalled what I killed, why I keep going back to the memory of the huge lizard, why I spent so much time as the great hunter.

The fact I found the lizard's body was turned over the day after I left it on its back, has something to do with the third eye. Perhaps, it made it easier for one last look at me. The third eye stood out from the decaying body the last time I saw it, a detail I missed until the final hunt. No other lizard I killed as a boy revealed a third eye to focus on me.

◆ ◆ ◆

The big lizard was the last one I killed. Somehow, my need to be a hunter ended. I found my BB gun rusting in the garage the following summer. Eventually, my mother threw it away.

The holes in the garage door are still there. Some of them contain old BB pellets that have found their place in the wood like remnants of an old western shootout. A few years ago, while visiting my family, I walked around the house and spotted the holes in the door. As I counted fourteen holes, I tried to think of a reason why I had loved to shoot lizards. What made me do it? Many of my friends shot birds. A couple of them got into trouble for hurting cats and dogs with their BB guns. I never shot birds or any other animal besides lizards. Were lizards acceptable because they were so abundant in the area? Was it human fear of monsters coming to get me? I rarely see them anymore when I visit the desert.

Absence of Lizards

I haven't seen a lizard
since I left the desert,
though I feel a lizard

behind my eyelids.
It darts in and out,
though I can't see it,
can't really picture it
jumping off a rock
to sit inside my head.

I recall the invasion
of the white lizards,
the season they beat
the desert rain, overflowed
into the arroyos,
sat on the adobe walls
like cut-off fingers,
twitching their tails,
waiting for me to approach
before leaping into
the cactus like torn pieces
of paper I threw away,
white lizards flashing
their mocking dance at me.

The last giant lizard I saw
was shot by a kid with a BB gun.
It was a foot-long,
dark-brown, thick, and fast.
The kid was a good shot
and left it in the dirt lot
across from my house.
I found it on my walk,
ants crawling over the rocks
to get to it, hundreds of them
opening the stiff, pregnant body
to get to the yellow eggs that
spilled out of its belly like
kernels of corn fertilizing
the hot sand.

Writing this poem and finding the twenty-five-year-old holes in the door unlocked the most important detail about the elusive lizard I finally killed. I have several recurring dreams about growing up in the desert. Most of the dreams involve images of old adobe ruins and cliff dwellings— stretches of hot ground crawling with dozens of enormous rattlesnakes, some sleeping entangled in each other, some poised to strike at me. When I dream of snakes, I wake up with no fear or anxiety, but I also wake with the memory of the third eye on the lizard. Somewhere, the lizards I killed as a boy watch me as snakes surround me in my dreams, but the lizards don't show themselves. Perhaps, I tried to erase it from my soul by giving up my ways as a hunter with a BB gun.

What does that say about us as predators? Can we truly forget? The huge lizard may be waiting for me to join it as it scurries across a field of tumbleweeds, fresh ground after a summer rain when the desert opens and hundreds of lizards, large and small, flash their tails before the arrogant hunter.

Haunted Adobe

My college roommate, Gary, and I lived in a haunted house along the Rio Grande. It was a four-room adobe rented for seventy dollars a month. It sat at the back of a huge parking lot adjoining La Hacienda, a popular Mexican restaurant in El Paso. A grove of old cottonwood trees gave us privacy from the dining crowds. The house stood twenty yards from an irrigation canal that ran parallel to the river, and it sat one hundred yards from the Mexican border at one of the busiest crossing points for thousands of illegals from Mexico.

We loved the little house and lived in it for two years. Graduate school is memorable, not for the studying and the term papers, but for the fun we had in that house. We partied, sat out on the porch in the evenings, wrote poems, and believed life along the river was paradise. It was one of the happiest times of my life—I was writing many poems and even worked on a failed novel. I had no idea it would be the end of my life in El Paso—the next year I would move to Denver, never to return to live in my hometown.

I could write a whole book on the house and that time, but the most memorable part was that the house was haunted. We were living in a very strange place.

This particular area of town is historically important. Old Fort Bliss, a cavalry outpost, still stands down the street and is used as low-income housing. Directly across the river from the house, a grove of cottonwoods, called

"The Peace Grove," marks the spot where Pancho Villa planted trees after the Battle of Juarez. And two miles north is an historical marker noting where the Spanish conquistador Don Juan de Oñate first crossed the Rio Grande, a journey that would change history and extend the conquest of the Americas begun by Cortés' genocide upon the inhabitants of Mexico City.

In between the parties and living the life of young poets, Gary and I noticed certain things about our house. Carita, his collie, would regularly bark at one corner of the living room. Most of the time, Carita acted normally, but quite often we would catch her growling at the empty spot where the two walls met, then she would become agitated and start barking. Gary and I would look in the corner, but nothing was there.

One night, upon closer inspection, Gary pointed to a dark spot on the ceiling directly above the corner. Since it was an old house, the walls were dirty, the paint peeling in places. The plaster roof was in good shape and the white paint looked like it had been applied in the last few years.

I looked up and saw a round, brown spot looking as if something had splashed onto the ceiling. It was fading and probably old.

"Dirt," I told him.

"A leak from the rain?" he wondered. What did it have to do with the dog always barking in that part of the room?

Since so many people from Mexico crossed the river behind the house, the area suffered from a high crime rate. The windows on the house had bars on them. It ruined the ancient feel of the house, but when we moved in, we were glad to have the bars as a way of keeping our stereos, albums, and books in the house.

The extreme security device was the bolted, wooden

front door. It was thick and heavy. Besides the dead bolts, the door had two rows of braces so we could slide wooden beams across it. Once we had locked ourselves in, we slid the beams across the door, then took pairs of huge nails and slipped them down the braces, locking the beams into place. We did this each night, removing the nails with a hammer in the morning. It was a pain, but we slept better knowing that that if anyone broke into the house, it was not likely to be through that door.

I slept in a bedroom at the north of the living room. Gary's room was on the southwest side. One night, after staying up late, we went through the door ritual, and then to bed. We weren't in our rooms more than half an hour when we both heard *it* at once.

As we lay in the quiet house, the scraping of the nails startled us as they rose off the braces.

"Gary!"

"What?" he answered across the house's darkness.

"Did you hear that?"

"Yeah."

Silence.

Again, we heard metal upon metal. We both got up and turned on our lamps at the same time. We came out into the living room and turned on the light. We went to the door— the bolts were still in the braces. The door was locked. Carita barked and barked at the door.

"You heard it," I whispered.

"Yeah. Did you?"

"Yeah."

Without saying it, we *knew* we had heard the bolts being lifted off the braces. We were used to the sound of scraping metal. The nails were at least five inches long and it took a good grip or use of the hammer to remove them.

The beams fit tightly and the metal always scraped loudly when we removed them.

"Someone pulled on them," Gary said.

"No way," I answered. "They're still there."

"I know that, but you heard it, right?"

"Yeah, we both heard it."

We went back to our rooms. The dog stopped barking. Neither of us slept well that night.

A few weeks later, I was having lunch with a friend I had met when we worked as substitute teachers in the El Paso public schools. I invited him to eat at La Hacienda after I told him where I lived. He knew the house right away and was eager to come by.

As we enjoyed our lunch, the subject of the old house and the grove of trees came up. He asked me if I liked living there. I told him that I did, then related the incident with the bolts.

"I'm not surprised," he said, smiling into his bowl of *menudo.*

"Why not?"

"Haven't you heard the story around here about the woman in the trees? I bet every waiter here knows it. My father's cousin used to work here, years ago, when it happened."

"What happened?" I almost didn't want to ask.

He smiled. "One day, three waiters were walking under those trees when they saw a woman dressed in black moving across the parking lot. The restaurant was already closed and there weren't any cars in the parking lot. They thought she was lost because she seemed to stop, hesitate, then kept walking in circles around the lot. They came out of the trees to talk to her, but before they could reach her, she disappeared."

"Disappeared? Are you serious?"

"Yeah."

"How could she disappear?"

"They said she just vanished when she got to the marker over there." He pointed to a stone monument connected to the historical Fort Bliss grounds.

"Are any of those waiters still working here," I asked and looked around.

"No, this was about twenty-five or thirty years ago. This is an old place. But my father used to tell me the story because his cousin worked here, even though he wasn't one of the three. He told my father two of the men quit after that because that vision of the woman scared them and made them think it was connected to the killing."

"What killing?" His way of revealing all these things to me in such a quiet, even tone amazed me. I stared into my menudo.

"You don't know about that either and you live in that house?" My friend looked stunned, but he smiled again.

"What don't we know?"

"A man was killed in that house. It happened a few years before the woman appeared in the trees. This Mexican used to work as a gateman."

"A gateman?"

"The house used to be a utility shed for the canal gates that control the water from the river. The guy used to live there and work the canal locks when it was irrigation time. This was before they built Elephant Butte Dam and the river was always deep and full. Somebody cut him into little pieces. They found parts of him in the canal and parts of him in the house."

"Did they find him in the front room?"

"I don't know. Why?" My friend was having a good time.

I told him about Carita's barking in the corner and the spot on the ceiling. But how could a spot of blood stay on the ceiling for over thirty years? The paint on the ceiling was not that old.

My friend told me that the man's murder and the woman in the trees were only two infamous stories about this part of El Paso. One of the oldest neighborhoods in El Paso, Sunset Heights, lay across Paisano Street, directly beyond the railroad tracks one mile from where we sat. Sunset Heights is made up of old houses, many designated historical landmarks. Some of them are huge two- or three-storey mansions, most of them having been renovated or repaired.

My friend said the next story took place when he was six years old. His parents bought a house in Sunset Heights, and moved in and fixed it up. But things started happening within weeks of the family's arrival.

One evening, while the whole family sat upstairs watching television, they were suddenly shaken by a thunderous bang downstairs. They ran down to the sound of breaking glass. They knew his mother's china cabinet was the only thing in the house that could make that much noise.

They ran into the dining room expecting to see the cabinet toppled over, but found the cabinet where it always had been. Not a single dish was broken. They checked every room, but did not find anything wrong. Again they were shaken by the vibration of something heavy falling downstairs, followed by the sound of breaking glass.

They never could keep a maid in the house. Maids refused to sleep in the basement room set aside for them; several of the Mexican women claimed that something pulled at their feet and hair when they tried to sleep at night.

My friend's parents saw an old man standing at the top of the stairs several times. Every now and then, as a family member walked around the house, one of them would feel something nudge them on the chin. My friend claims it happened to him once. He felt a cold finger push at his chin.

The final straw came one night when his parents were asleep. Their bedroom suddenly turned cold and they woke up. When his father turned on the light, the two of them saw the marks of a weight pushing down on the deep carpet. The marks moved slowly toward the bed, only to disappear before reaching them.

"We moved out of the house after two months of this happening," he said. "After we had found a peaceful house in another part of town, my mother went down to the City and County Building to look up old city records. In her research, she discovered that the whole block of houses was built on the old Fort Bliss cemetery."

He ended in a quiet voice and just looked at me. I didn't say anything, but gazed out the large bay windows of the restaurant toward the house where I lived.

In the two years that Gary and I stayed there, we never heard those bolts again, and we never saw a woman in the trees. Even though we loved living there, the house gave us a strange feeling between surreal peace and a nervous, deceptive feeling that something lay hidden in those tiny rooms. Carita always barked at the corner. We gave up trying to figure out the spot on the ceiling.

A few years later, after moving to Denver, I returned to El Paso and drove by the restaurant. When I pulled into the parking lot, I saw that our adobe house had been torn down. But the rubble had not been removed. Weeds and bushes grew through the piles of brick.

I think of those two years fondly and wish I could capture everything that took place in the house. It was a magical time of discovering poetry, finishing school, walking along the river, spending special times with friends. I never thought I would say good-bye to twenty-five years of living along the Rio Grande, an area hiding many secrets, daring its sons to return and dig through piles of bricks to see if anything was left behind.

Taos, 1977

It is my first time in Taos Pueblo and I am left with a sick feeling, an anger I never knew I had, an unexpected shame. I found the Taos Pueblo beneath the shadow of snowy Taos Mountain, adobes of spirit and hard history overrun by tourists, and cars with license plates of many colors. I watched dozens of families pull up to the ticket booth for a two-dollar tour of the only Anasazi-style community still occupied on the North American continent, five- and six-storey houses clustered together, the pueblo founded over five hundred years ago.

One must pay to enter the pueblo. Why did I join these crowds in gawking and staring at the Taos people, the ghost-like inhabitants who walked slowly over the dirt streets? The tourists around me stared, and I stared. Then I stared at the tourists. An occasional click of a camera would break the silence, but most of the tourists were so awestruck by the chance to look back in time that they kept their numerous cameras strung around their necks.

Even though I grew up in the desert Southwest, I was never really aware of the destruction of the Indian way of life until this first visit to Taos. I grew up in such an internal, closed world of my surrounding desert, I had no idea of how older, native cultures lived in the area. I had read countless books on Western history, but none of them portrayed what this scene revealed. Not only was I witnessing it for the first time, I participated by staring at the Taos women draped in their brown robes, their faces covered like Arabic women. They dragged themselves along the adobe walls, walked closely to the tall buildings to disappear beyond mud corners into the mystery of the houses. I saw the cultural and psychological damage committed by American tourists with cameras and guide maps, gawking at the native people like they were animals in a zoo.

My own feelings of awe and revulsion clashed, pulled through me by the stunning beauty of the mountains surrounding Taos and by the deep mystery of the ancient buildings, dwellings that seemed to melt into the earth as I stood back and took in the whole panorama.

Taos Pueblo is surrounded on the north and south by an eroding adobe wall. Although it could easily be breached and climbed, it serves as a kind of cultural barrier against the outside world, but is ineffective against the tourist tide. The whole pueblo is dominated by walls and mud barriers. It is the people's way of keeping things in and out for centuries; yet the earth is in the constant battle for providing adobe for shelter as adobe erodes in the sun and rain. Taos people believe so much in these walls that electricity is banned within the low wall. Any design change is governed by the pueblo council. Members of the pueblo must get permission even to cut new windows.

This sense of building from the earth, of surrounding yourself with mud and giving in to it, is best exemplified by the enormous earthen mounds outside the perimeter of the main wall. Two of the huge mounds rise a few yards from the tourist entrance. When I found out what they were, I wondered why they had been left so close to the areas open to outsiders.

There are four mounds called "ash piles" around the pueblo. I thought they were trash dumps, but my later reading revealed the significance of these mounds. The Taos people put in broken shards, broken implements, and anything else they swept out of their houses. These are examples of what these people thought was good in the world. They even placed prayer offerings on top of the dumps during ceremonial occasions.

I sensed that we were witnessing an earthy existence giving in to invasion. It was the centuries-old struggle to live within the earth and tower above it, while the walls disintegrated because they could not hold up any longer. Now, instead of accepting the remains of everyday existence into the mounds, the Taos people were probably sweeping ticket receipts and empty Kodak cartons into the mud, wondering what kind of results the earth would give back to them as they pushed the remains of outsiders into holy ground.

The pueblo tries to make you feel good about coming here. And, why not? New Mexico depends on tourists dollars for a large part of its economy. In the land of enchantment, it is romantic to see the pueblos and search for the country that Georgia O'Keeffe painted and D. H. Lawrence wrote about. (His ashes are buried on a mountain near Taos.)

The Taos people sell bread and souvenirs to the tourists. This means entering deeper into the town and crossing the central plaza, an area regarded as sanctified space for centuries. I moved across the plaza and crossed a narrow bridge over Red Willow Creek, the community's only source of drinking and washing water. It also connects the pueblo to its sacred Blue Lake, hidden from view behind the mountain.

Some of the adobe apartments on the other side of the creek had been turned into a bread store and souvenir shops. Groups of tourists walked out of the attractive little shops with chunks of Indian bread in their hands and sparkling turquoise weighing down their fingers and necks.

Inside the bread store, I bought a loaf of the delicious bread. The Indian who waited on me was a young, quiet boy, maybe twelve or thirteen. He had long black hair tied in a ponytail and wore a red bandanna around his head. He was dressed in Levi's with a green Western shirt and jacket. A huge turquoise ring sparkled on his right hand.

I gave him the money for the bread without saying a word. He looked at me with a blank expression and handed me the loaf wrapped in a plastic bag. Behind the counter, there were trays of bread on a small table. I could smell the freshness of it from the tiny kitchen in the back room where three Taos women rolled and cooked the bread in modern ovens.

I nodded thanks to the boy and walked out of the simple shop, its long counter piled with bread, the walls bare, no sign of tourist attractions save for the boy dressed to the hilt in Western clothes and noticeable jewelry. Did his clothes bring more money from bread buyers? I bought the bread because I wanted to complete the process of intrusion and try to come to terms with the grief and power of it, how the Taos people had given in to this profit as an obvious means of support and survival. The bread was delicious, a small loaf I ate quickly.

I crossed the bridge back over the icy water and pulled the entrance stub from my pocket. It was my legal pass to enter and study the magnificent architecture of brown earth and mud. I watched four women and children draw water from the creek in large clay jars. They lifted the jars heavily onto their shoulders and made their way across the earthen plaza, their daily routine open to those who studied them and perhaps dreamed of being them in another time, hearts drawn to the romance of the West.

On ceremonial days, the plaza becomes the stage for dancing and praying. One far area of the plaza seemed closed to the tourists who wandered about. I walked toward that corner of the buildings and stopped in front of a sign— "Closed to the Public."

Beyond the sign, set back from direct view, but detectable from the plaza by their ladder poles, are Taos' six active *kivas,* underground chambers or rooms, usually round and accessible only by a narrow opening in the ceiling. North-side kivas are within the community wall surrounded by unusual wood fences encircling the ladder housing; the three south-side kivas are outside the wall with masonry enclosing their hatchways.

The kivas function on secrecy. Unlike most Pueblo Indians, Taos people base their political and social organization on kiva allegiance. There is no strong clan allegiance as found in other pueblos. Each child is "given" to one of these kivas at adolescence and is introduced by priests to the responsibilities of the pueblo.

That these kivas were underground reinforced my sense that I was in the middle of an earthy existence, a way of life dissolving into the ground at the same time that its ancient houses towered in the New Mexico sun. Their evolution back to dirt was mutated by the intrusion of the outside world, which sets its own rules for visiting the pueblo, tourism bringing money to the state and the bread bakers, perhaps even to the elders who kept tourists away from the kivas.

As I walked away from the off-limits area, I saw a couple of bony, yellow dogs staring at me from their posts near closed doorways. They growled but didn't move. All the doors to the houses were kept shut, every window blocked by pieces of wood or pieces of colored cloth.

I noticed another sign warning that most of the pueblo was off limits, and that it was prohibited to bother any of the people, except those working in the shops. I wanted the sign to make me feel better. It didn't. I moved next to a group of tourists with cameras poised in their hands, waiting and searching for something worth shooting.

I watched one couple click off several shots of the buildings. They spotted an old woman coming out of her house. She went to one of the clay ovens that rose out of the ground in front of her doorway. When she bent over to get something from inside the oven, they took more pictures. I could not see what the old woman withdrew from the oven. There was no sign of smoke or smells of cooking in the clay. She bundled a tiny object in her shawl and quickly disappeared inside the building.

I couldn't stay any longer, the confusing guilt of being in the pueblo returning to drive me back to my car. As I walked across the plaza, I noticed a break in the adobe wall that surrounded it. I turned and noticed a similar break in the opposite wall and realized that these were the openings for the Sun Road I had heard about.

The Sun Road is a sacred space linking Taos to the cosmos in an unmarked east-to-west racetrack. Running for a quarter-mile from the plaza through the breaks in the wall, the Sun Road symbolizes the path the sun follows through the sky each winter. In the fall and spring, ceremonial runners initiate relay races to lend their strength to the sun, so that it makes it through the long season. Unfortunately, these sacred spaces can be overlooked by modern people wanting to upgrade the attraction of the pueblos and other Indian communities. When a road was proposed from the nearby Rancho de Taos development to the pueblo, Taos leaders refused because it would have destroyed an ancient Sun Road.

As I stared at the breaks in the wall, then looked up at the sun hidden by thick clouds, I knew something had changed within me. Although I did not know it at that moment, I would leave the area for good a year later.

On the way back to my car, I turned to look at the mountains beyond Taos. The sky was a deep blue above snow peaks that capped the brown and purple cliffs. A thin haze crossed Taos Mountain, close to the pine trees growing together like deep-green bruises against the mountainside, covering the secret paths to Blue Lake. Every August, the people from the Taos Pueblo make a pilgrimage to Blue Lake. Songs are sung and prayer sticks are planted where the Natives believe human beings first emerged from the earth.

I wanted to go there to be alone, but that form of earth did not belong to me. My cave was not there. My entrance to and exit from the world was not to be found at Blue Lake. I wanted to go to Taos Mountain to get away from this pueblo filled with Americans trying to recapture a time and place their human lives could never give them—not even to a native Southwesterner like me. I wanted to go to the mountain to pass my shame for entering this pueblo, but also to put the guilt in perspective against my own Chicano ancestry, a *mestizo* tale of Indian and Spanish blood I didn't know much about, never having bothered to investigate it despite my life in the area.

Living in the twentieth century and rapidly approaching the twenty-first, I did not know how to find my own family story completely. As a writer, I had attempted it without total satisfaction. Perhaps this is why so many people are drawn to the ancient pueblos, hoping their visits will awaken something within them that may answer personal mysteries, give them stronger reasons for accepting their existence in their own towns.

I knew the tourists would never find what they were trying to capture by coming here. They couldn't do it by staring at people living their simple lives among adobe that has absorbed the New Mexico sun for centuries, creating birth and death out of the muddy earth while holding its own secrets of Western history that no American will discover, no historian analyze, and no writer create with words.

I headed for the D. H. Lawrence shrine in the mountains beyond Taos, going to visit a writer who had also tried to understand, but had left his ashes instead. I drove out of the pueblo gate, a path burning to be left alone to crumble and erode into invisibility and its underground sources, returning to the earth on its given time under the Sun Road.

PART TWO

White Sands

It was like playing on the moon as we rolled down the white sand dunes when we were kids. By the time we came to a stop at the bottom, we were covered in white dirt, looking like ghost children. The memory of family picnics at the White Sands National Monument near Alamogordo, New Mexico, in the fifties is blurred now, but I still cling to a few vivid images of miles and miles of a white world where I had fun playing in the dunes, building white sand castles without knowing we were only a few miles from the government test site where Trinity, the first atomic bomb, was detonated on July 16, 1945.

Until I studied World War II in high school, I did not know the white desert playground of the park distracted visitors from the fact that they were near the historic site. After seeing what I was reading, my mother casually told me that she and my father, along with thousands of El Pasoans, had seen a bright flash in the sky on July 16. My parents were high school students at El Paso Technical when the test bomb went off one hundred miles to the north. No one knew what the flash was until years later, but she told me that day felt very unusual. The sudden light made many people nervous because the war was still on.

My parents had witnessed a turning point in history by seeing that bright light in the sky. As a child, I spent many weekends playing in the white sands of the future, just another kid amazed at the endless horizon of white hills and

dunes, the light falling from the desert sun to wither everything in 95-degree heat, making us play harder as the light
intensified.

I can't forget the first day we walked through the park
museum. Besides the usual geological charts and raised
maps, I saw displays of mounted white mice, white rabbits,
and white coyotes—even white tarantulas. These creatures
had adjusted to this white world so that they could survive
in the heat and desolation of the bleached landscape. Each
species evolved to take advantage of an endless camouflage.
When I learned about Trinity, I wondered how many of the
animals had been affected by the radiation of history. Had
they truly changed color to blend into the white sand for
protection and survival against predators, or was this ivory
land, and its creatures, a mutation from the first blast?

Concerns over nuclear fallout were not hot topics for
high school students in an isolated, west Texas town during
the sixties. No one thought about it. It was not an issue.
I knew nature had created the white sands thousands of
years ago and the evolution of white animals had nothing to
do with the atomic bomb, but as I remembered that day in
the museum, I sensed the whiteness of every living thing
around me was connected to the darkness of the brilliant
flash of 1945.

I first read Leslie Groves' eyewitness account of the Alamogordo explosion when my American History class studied the development of the atomic bombs the U.S. dropped
on Hiroshima and Nagasaki. As director of the Manhattan Project, a top-secret government program, Groves described what he saw across the white sands as an intense and
blinding flash of light, a tremendous ball of fire that turned
into the first mushroom cloud that any of them saw. He
watched as the steel tower vaporized in the 15,000 to 20,000

tons of explosives.

When I read this in high school and recognized the area as the place we enjoyed family outings, I had not been to White Sands in years. Groves' account did not really strike me until a decade later. In high school, it was just another assigned chapter to read. For whatever reasons, my high school friends and I never went to White Sands, even though it was less than two hours from El Paso. I enjoyed the white fields only as a small boy.

I didn't make the connection between the bomb, my parents seeing the flash, and my naive childhood in the sand until 1977, as I drove alone across southern New Mexico. I was on my way back to El Paso after living for two years in San Diego, California. I drove south past Albuquerque. But instead of taking the straight, short route to El Paso, I headed east from Las Cruces over the Organ Mountains.

The high pass took me to the eastern side of the range, directly above the vast flatness of the desert floor and White Sands, forty miles away. I don't know why I chose to return to El Paso from that direction, but driving past White Sands brought it all back. Perhaps I thought of those days because friends of mine in San Diego had mentioned their participation in antinuclear groups protesting at the nuclear power plant near San Clemente. The last demonstration had taken place a few days before I said good-bye to them and headed home.

It was an early evening in April when I headed down the long stretch of highway bordering the eastern end of White Sands. The setting sun ignited the peaks of the Organ Mountains and washed the miles of white sand with a peach-colored hue. I drove past fenced-off land whose barbed-wired barriers held small signs every few hundred feet. "Property of United States Government. No Trespassing."

A simple warning like that was enough to keep people away and draw them to the park instead. Thousands of visitors came each year to gawk at the white sand dunes, miles and miles of them. Roads had been cut to get into the interior dunes. After the shock of the white world wore off, families could eat at the picnic tables scattered throughout the park.

I spotted the museum building about a mile down the road and began to relive our family picnics. It must have been 1958. As a six-year-old, I thrilled in climbing the steep dunes to pretend I was going to get lost out there and scare my parents into coming to look for me. When I stood at the top of the dunes, my father and mother looked tiny and far away as they sat at the picnic table at the bottom.

I waved and yelled until I caught their attention. They waved back, but I couldn't hear what they were saying. I turned and started hiking across the deep sand. The white powder seeped into my sneakers and pant cuffs. I never hiked more than a hundred yards before I began to get scared at the realization that I was standing in an endless sea of whiteness. I would turn and retrace my deep footprints back to the family.

Now, as I drove past the museum, I had the urge to stop and find out if the display of white animals was still there. I slowed down and saw the "Closed" sign on the doors. Twenty years after my first visit to the museum, I couldn't go in to look at the white kangaroo rats, the snarling white coyote, or the huge albino rattlesnake that was the most vivid, shocking animal mounted in the museum.

I sped past the closed building and continued toward El Paso, remembering how the white rattlesnake had startled me as a boy. After peering into the glass-enclosed exhibits of rats and lizards, I came upon the coiled body of the rattlesnake. The sight of a white reptile, and the fact that it had come from the sands where I loved to play, increased my wonder and was one of the first times I felt I belonged in the desert.

My nose barely cleared the top of the display, so I had to stand on tiptoe to get a good look. I stared at the huge snake and couldn't believe the sight of its pale skin and transparent rattler. Its head was a dirty, milky white with tiny black eyes, the only dark spots on the body. I had seen rattlesnakes in El Paso, but I never guessed they could turn white to live in these sands.

The rest of that day is a blur. I think I ran out of the museum to find my parents and sister walking back to the picnic area. I didn't say a word to them about the white rattlesnake. I sat at the table and kept looking up at the walls of white sand as we ate, wondering if I had rolled over any snakes in my adventures in the dunes. I can still see the sudden brightness of the white sand as it intensified while we ate. It must have been noon on a hot day because I see myself sitting at the table, sweating and biting into my sandwich as the blinding sunlight draws the white earth closer to me.

◆ ◆ ◆

I drove toward El Paso and the heat of the picnic faded. I couldn't recall the last time my family took me to White Sands. As I approached Alamogordo, the image of the white rattlesnake changed from a coiled shape to a mushroom cloud rising above the desert.

I have never been an antinuclear activist or protester, and have never even read books about Hiroshima, but as I drove through the area where Trinity was detonated, I thought about those childhood picnics, the white animals in the museum, and the brilliance of the sands. I discovered a certain light, a clarity of understanding, a radiance burning through the dunes of family history.

Its energy came from many sources. The innocence of childhood produced the light on those white hills. Our family outings generated the heat because they were part of growing up with a sense that the concept of family could never be broken. Those picnics on the dunes represented the idealism of a small boy growing up in the late fifties, a boy who thought the world was made up of nothing but good times.

The energy of the blinding desert also came from the fact that the U.S. government chose this area in which to conduct experiments that would change world history. If someone had interrupted my fun on the dunes to tell me that the Manhattan Project had reached its climax a few miles away, I couldn't have comprehended it. As a child, I would have thought the idea of a big bomb in the desert was kind of neat. Nothing could have destroyed my playground.

Twelve years after my solitary drive past the dunes toward home, the first test of a Star Wars laser weapon was successfully completed at White Sands. In 1989, the U.S. government finally shot down a missile with a laser. The flight and destruction of the missile took place over White Sands. Forty-four years after the first atomic flash startled the people of El Paso, another turning point had taken place over the white dunes.

As before, the energy for the laser weapon came from the white desert, from energy spilling over from the atomic bomb. Yet it was a power derived from the desert itself.

In *Masked Gods* (Swallow Press, 1984), his classic book on Navajo history, Frank Waters writes about the *kiva* ceremonies of native people and he reflects on the future of mankind and how studying native religions gives many clues to our turbulent century.

He describes a visit to Los Alamos, the town near Santa Fe founded in 1945 to house scientists working on the Manhattan Project. The atomic reactor constructed there was named Clementine after the miner's daughter of the folk song. Waters states that the Clementines were also an Egyptian religious sect in the first century A.D. who believed in the female spirit. He compares this female power to the same force rising out of the kivas near Los Alamos. He points out that the Sun Temple at Mesa Verde is the most intense example because elaborate ceremonies of light and fire were held there, ceremonies to end life cycles and begin new ones, the whole process forming out of the sheer power of Mother Earth and her underground forces.

Waters writes about the Sun Temple of Mesa Verde and its parallel to the atomic reactor. He feels it is not far-fetched to see the parallel in their meanings. He compares the physical energy locked inside the atom to the psychic energy inside our psyches. They both involve the transformation of matter into creative energy. This creation arises from a dependence on what he calls "the reconciliation" of the primitive forces of life. This fusion results in a new birth of energy.

Tremendous conflict—from the smallest, insignificant act of a small boy rolling down the white dunes, to Trinity exploding nearby—detonates past the spiritual kivas toward the end of the twentieth century and the Stars Wars forming high above the desert. If Frank Waters is correct, and if the white rattlesnake is my most vivid memory of the White Sands museum, then the first atomic blast that startled my parents was destined to take place in the desert of New Mexico. It is a transcendence of light from the ancient

people to the builders of the test tower melting at ground
zero, to me rolling down the white dunes as rattlesnakes
coiled undetected nearby—all the way to the final act of
driving past the closed museum.

✦ ✦ ✦

As I drove past Alamogordo and neared El Paso, the
white sands were left behind. The familiar brown and red
desert covered the horizon. To my right, the Franklin
Mountains rose in a purple haze. I was coming home to
again live in El Paso.

I made my way through the northeast suburbs of my
home town and tried to picture what it must have been like
to see the flash on July 16, 1945. My mother said it lasted
only an instant and life went on. I stared at the mountains
and noticed how new housing developments were creeping
up the canyons. It meant cutting into the desert, disrupting
the ancient landscape, uprooting cactus, and forcing wild-
life to readjust. It also meant that many new homeowners in
the foothills of the Franklins would find rattlesnakes in
their yards. I wondered how many they would kill, or if any
of those people in the new suburbs would get bitten. It was
a small ecological problem. The snakes would disappear.

I drove into El Paso knowing that none of those homeowners would ever be startled or frightened by a white
rattlesnake. They would never learn albino rattlesnakes
lived one hundred miles to the north of their new homes.
These new residents of El Paso had no reason to discover
the secrets that lay hidden in their magnificent desert. It
was too vast, too much property. They would have no urge
to explore beyond the city limits of their dreams. Retirees
from nearby military installations and new high-tech company employees weren't interested in local history. It's not

part of the dream. After all, the stark, brown mountains a few miles from their backyards gave off a beautiful light each evening, enough heat to satisfy them in their moment under the Southwest sun.

Peace Grove

The last house where I lived in El Paso was one mile from the Peace Grove, the cottonwoods Pancho Villa planted on the Mexican side of the Rio Grande near Juarez, where his rebel troops fought government soldiers in 1911. The battle lasted two days and was witnessed by hundreds of El Pasoans who camped along the river to watch. The Peace Grove was Villa's way of showing there could be peace, that the bloody Mexican Revolution could end. But the planting of the trees may have also been a signal to the U.S. and General John Pershing to leave the Mexicans alone to fight their own war. Even though they captured Juarez, Villa's army did not stay long. Two days later, they headed south into Chihuahua to continue the fight.

The idea of a revolutionary planting trees and the fact that the trees are standing today intrigued me when I lived in a tiny adobe house on the border of the two countries. From that house, one hundred yards from the Rio Grande, I saw thousands of illegal aliens, or as some of them preferred to be called, *mojados,* cross into the U.S. I stared every day at the crumbling huts of the Juarez *colonias* across the river.

The area behind my house was a favorite crossing point because the Rio Grande was very shallow west of downtown El Paso. The U.S. Border Patrol could not keep Mexicans out despite their constant patrolling of the area. The Peace Grove stood between the river and the low hills on the west end of Juarez, its neat rows of trees in sharp contrast to the decaying streets and houses, the broken walls painted turquoise, yellow, purple, or pink. The vast poverty and squalor spread for miles, blessed by the enduring limbs of the Peace Grove.

One evening after a sudden thunderstorm had rolled up from the south and swept through El Paso, I went for a walk on the levee road above the irrigation canal. It paralleled the river on the U.S. side. The black clouds moved slowly to the west and their bottom layers turned pink in the setting sun. Despite the heavy rain, the Rio Grande was nearly dry. It flowed in slow, muddy trails. As I walked south, I looked across the river at the cottonwoods and thought about my grandfather, Bonifacio Canales, who fought for Villa in the battle for Juarez. It was the only fighting he did during the revolution. He and my grandmother Julia had just been married. They were both fourteen years old and had fled Chihuahua for the border. When Villa's men entered Juarez, young *campesinos* chose sides, most of them deciding to help Villa take the town. After the victorious rebel army left, my grandparents fled to Arizona, where Bonifacio worked for the railroad in the Yaqui Indian labor camps until too much alcohol brought his early death in 1941.

I wondered what the young boys who fought for Villa thought about planting trees. Did anyone try to destroy the grove after Villa's departure? Did any of the rebels ever return to Juarez to see if the trees had grown? The rebels reminded me of several friends who had gone to Nicaragua in 1985, after the Sandinista Revolution, to show their support by joining local work brigades in planting trees in the war-torn country. They told me how U.S.–backed Contras later destroyed many of the crops in the countryside and burned the young trees the Americans had planted.

My thoughts were interrupted by the sound of tires screeching on gravel. I looked behind me at the Border Patrol car that pulled up in a frantic spin. The officer leaped out of the lime-green car and pointed a finger at me. "Hey, you wetback!" the Anglo officer sneered. "Got you, again!"

"Are you talking to me, Officer?" I smiled and spoke in my clearest Texas drawl. Yes, Chicanos can have good Texas accents when they want to.

"You speak English?" He approached with one hand on his holstered gun. He wore tiny sunglasses and sported a crewcut. He looked like he was in his early twenties.

"Yes. I probably speak it better than you."

He stood in front of me with his hands on his hips, uncertain what to do next. As we stared at each other, I could hear someone speaking Spanish across the river and the busy humming of traffic on Paisano Street to my right.

"You look like a wetback to me. Got any I.D.?"

I looked around to see if there were any potential witnesses nearby, but no one else was in sight. "Yes, I have a driver's license, but I don't think I have to show it to you, since I am an American citizen."

No muscle moved on the stony face behind the sunglasses. "Where do you live?"

I pointed to my house one hundred yards down the road. "Over there."

We both heard the squawking of his car radio and we stared at each other. "Yeah, I've seen you around here. Any wetbacks cross here?" He shook his head toward the river.

I shrugged and didn't answer. He shook his head again and walked briskly to his car. He gave me another look and climbed in. He pulled into reverse, made another loud turn on the narrow road, and screeched away in a thick trail of dust. I watched the car disappear around a bend, and then

saw four Mexicans run across the road. They had been
crouching behind the tall salt cedars that lined the street.
They climbed the embankment and quickly vanished on
Paisano toward downtown.

I laughed, but was angry. It was not the first time I had
been stopped by the Border Patrol. They probably did have
the right to ask for my I.D., but they usually backed down
once they discovered that the brown-skinned person they
were questioning was an English-speaking U.S. citizen who
could report them to their superiors. I had called Border
Patrol headquarters once when a patrol car pulled me and a
friend over for no reason. The two officers stuck flashlights
in our faces, didn't say a word to us, and drove off into the
night. I reported them, but of course nothing happened.

I tried to forget this latest confrontation and kept walking to get a better view of the Peace Grove. I stopped another fifty yards down the road and looked across the river.
The final light from the setting sun hit the trees and out-
lined them in orange. The combination of sunset and distant rain clouds cast a dark, burning glow over the western
sky and washed over the Juarez colonias, making the houses
look like they were on fire. I spotted a few people climbing
the dirt streets to disappear over the tops of the hills. Several dogs barked and ran among the garbage that lay in the
streets closest to the river.

I sat on the embankment of the levee road and watched
the whole area turn darker. The river sparkled but barely
moved. Its mud stretched in long layers of smooth sand for
hundreds of yards. As I sat on the border of the two countries, watching the still group of full cottonwoods with their
huge leaves, I realized that there was no border. Pancho
Villa had planted those trees directly across from where I
sat because that is where events dictated he should plant

them. The two dozen trees, standing tall and healthy along the river, found their spot near the water because the line had been drawn there. It had been decided decades ago. No Mexican Revolution and no constant prowling of Border Patrol cars, nor the fact that thousands of people crossed this spot illegally, could affect the way the trees grew. They had no say in which direction the roots had spread since 1911.

I felt exhilarated and wanted to dig under the river with my bare hands to find the roots of the trees spreading across the river, covering this side. I wanted to know that the trees would absorb so much water that, sooner or later, they would dry the river, making the riverbed disappear. Then there would be no sign of a border! I wanted to see horses and Villa's troops digging to stick young trees into the mud across from me. I wanted to find El Pasoans sitting on the bank, having a good time, watching the planting instead of acting like war was a sporting event to watch, pass judgment on, then interfere with. I didn't know all the historical details behind the planting of the trees. My thoughts of roots coming toward me, underground, wiping out the levee road and the patrol cars, blended with the last light of the evening.

I heard a splash in the water, but could not see anything in the river. Smoke from wood stoves and an occasional electric light dotted the hills of the colonias. I rose and started to walk home, then heard angry voices across the river. I could barely make out two running figures as they moved through the Peace Grove. One of them shouted something I couldn't understand, and the angry voice of a woman replied, "*¡Vamonos! ¡Vamonos!*"

They stopped under a tree and argued in loud voices. The second figure was a man who tugged at the woman's dress. She shook him off, stepped a few feet back, and yelled something at him. He threw up his hands and joined her. They approached the river and began to wade across.

I turned away and headed home. When I reached the bend in the levee, I paused and looked for them. They crouched in the middle of the low river, two more waiting to enter, watching for *la migra*. I didn't see any patrol cars. The couple ran the rest of the way and blended into the darkness on this side. I kept walking, then heard a car engine start. The headlights of a patrol car blinded me and blocked my path. I stopped and waited for the officer, a different one this time, to get out and question me. I knew this meant I was going to take my time getting back to my house along the Rio Grande.

Crossing to America

He knocked on my door at two o'clock in the morning. The wind blew hard on that cold January night. The knocking startled me and I woke up quickly. I thought one of the cottonwoods had fallen against the porch. I got up and went to the window in the front room of the adobe house. The full moon over the border blinked through the black clouds, the trees swaying madly in the yard. I saw the figure on the porch.

"Who is it?"

"*¡Amigo! ¡Ayudame!*"

I hesitated to open the door. Too many strangers crossed my house, its isolated spot near the Rio Grande a good place for illegal aliens to cross the border from Mexico.

"*¿Qué quieres?*" I looked at him through the window, but the howling wind kept me from hearing what he said. The figure wrapped his arms tightly around his chest. As my eyes got accustomed to the night, I saw he was a young Mexicano, probably a *mojado,* as they called themselves. He had nothing to keep him warm except old pants and a torn T-shirt.

I opened the door to find him shivering in the winter night. He was dripping wet. His whole body shook. His eyes widened for an instant, and then looked helplessly down at the ground.

"*Una camisa.*"

"¿Qué?"

"Una camisa." He patted his wet shoulders and asked me for a shirt. I didn't know what to do. This was the first time one of them had come to my door to ask for something. They usually crossed the river and disappeared toward downtown El Paso as fast as they could, the Border Patrol catching a few and missing thousands a month.

As cold as it was in the January air, I knew he was freezing. He must have fallen into the ten-foot deep canal behind the house after crossing the shallow river.

"Entra." I opened the door.

He shook his head, the wet hair clinging to his forehead. *"Una camisa, por favor."*

I wanted him to come in and get out of the chilling wind, but he refused. All he wanted was a dry shirt to wear. I turned the lamp on in the room and went to my closet. I found an old, thick wool shirt too small for me and quickly brought it to him. On the way, I grabbed a blanket from the bed.

His body kept shaking, the wet clothes glistening against his thin body, his hair wet and wild looking, his deep brown face fighting the shock of the wind, holding on to the last hesitation of pride that would not allow him to enter the warm house. The cold rushed into the room and I shivered.

"Hace mucho frío. Entra." I held up the blanket, but he shook his head again.

"La camisa."

All he wanted was the shirt, so I gave it to him. He tore it from my hands, peeled off the wet T-shirt and put on the dry one.

"¿Por qué no entras? ¿Quieres café?" I offered to make him some coffee.

I held the door against the freezing wind, but he still

refused to come in. The trees shook louder, their bare branches black veins against the moonlight. I felt sorry for the young man and wanted to help him get warm, but I couldn't understand why he would not come into my house. He started to walk away. *"Gracias, señor."*

"¡Vente! ¡Entra!" I pleaded with him and wondered if he would catch pneumonia. What would happen to him in the winter night?

He shook his head, ran across the yard into the grove of black cottonwoods. *"Ya estóy en los Estados Unidos. ¡Ya estóy aquí!"* he yelled.

He was already where he wanted to be. Before I could say *"adiós,"* he ran into the trees and disappeared in the direction of Paisano Street, the first dry path one takes when crossing into America.

Without Discovery

When I was in elementary school in El Paso in the fifties and sixties, we studied American historical icons like Davy Crockett, Abraham Lincoln, and Christopher Columbus. The heroic importance of historical characters like Crockett and Lincoln were obvious to a daydreaming boy like myself. I always wanted to be a hero and created my own characters in the strange little stories I wrote in my spiral-bound notebook.

Columbus was something else, though. It was harder for me to understand what my history and social studies teachers were saying when they told my classmates and me that Columbus sailed in three ships and discovered where we lived. How could anyone discover El Paso, Texas, and the United States when they had always been here? I didn't understand how people in the fifteenth century couldn't know the United States was here. When it finally hit me, I realized Columbus was a great hero because he discovered a wild land full of savage Indians, the bad guys who killed many explorers like Columbus and fought to keep my country from ever being created.

In the fifth grade, I added Columbus to my list of heroes, and even made up my own stories of exploration where my friends and I sailed down the Rio Grande in wooden rafts we built in my backyard, bound for those narrow, sandy islands that stuck out in the middle of the dry river. We never actually did anything like that, but when the whole

concept of exploration and discovery finally sunk in, I knew
heroes like Crockett and Lincoln could not have performed
their mighty deeds without Columbus coming along to get
the whole thing started. This guy with his *Niña, Pinta,* and
Santa María was our true leader and he must have been a
brave man taking on so many red-skinned Indians.

I can still see those colorful illustrations in my history
textbook, the bearded and armored Spaniards taking on the
dark painted, half-naked hordes of savages. My friends and
I didn't play cowboys and Indians for nothing. We knew
who the good guys were, even though a cowboy hat and a
shiny gun and holster were more fun than weird armored
helmets and long swords. I got stuck being one of the Indians because, when sides were drawn on the playground, the
few Chicanos who went to Putnam Elementary were told
they were the Indians. I rarely got to be one of the good
guys.

I did a report on Columbus' three ships and got an A+
on it. I was a good artist and spent a great deal of time drawing the intricate sails on the ships. I knew everything about
them, and my fifth grade teacher was pleased. That A+ told
me I was an explorer, and I knew the history of my country.
I understood all about good and evil, how the story of us all
was clearly written and told in the textbooks I loved to take
home and read. No one had to force me to do homework.
My fascination with explorers pushed me to read more and
find those books in the library that told me the Mexicans
who killed Davy Crockett at the Alamo were blood-thirsty,
dumb peasants, that our proud forefathers settled the West
because those same tribes of people who resisted Columbus were keeping cities like El Paso from being established.

When I was forced to play Indian at school, I resigned
myself to it, though I felt shamed and hoped that not too

many of my teachers would see me on the playground and wonder why this student, who was so good at re-creating the voyage of Columbus, was whooping and hollering on the monkey bars. At times, I was afraid they would not let me do another report on the good guys because I was some kind of traitor on the playground. The other boys had the wooden pistols and the cowboy hats. I had nothing except my hand over my mouth, hollering and jumping like an Indian, waiting for the tougher kids to run around the swing set and shoot me.

By the time the bell rang to go to class, all the Indians had to roll in the dirt and play dead. If you got up, the cowboys would kick you or throw dirt at you. As the Indians, guys like Carlos Uranga, Sammy Madrid, and myself were always the last ones to walk into class. The cowboys got to go in first. That is the way it was, and my fascination with Columbus and his three ships took on a secret role in my world of heroes because I had to be an Indian on the playground. My A+ didn't mean anything outside the classroom.

My later years in high school were often marked by extreme incidents of racism against me and the few Chicanos who went to Coronado High School. I got used to being called "dumb Mexican," hearing the jokes about "wetbacks," being left out of projects with other students, being assaulted for being so quiet and "greasy." The racism influenced the beginning of my life of silence, where my heroes had been replaced with a desire to write and create my own worlds. As an avid reader, I began to discover the truth behind the myths of Crockett and Columbus. Yet, the story of genocide against native people has taken me a lifetime to come to terms with and try to understand. I have yet to truly study and comprehend the impact of Hernán Cortés burning the Aztec civilization and Mexico City to the ground, fusing it into my own mestizo family lines that have a great deal to do with how Chicanos and other Hispanics should look at these last five hundred years.

Growing up in Texas made me aware of the long, bloody history of oppression against Mexican Americans. Moving to San Antonio recently, and going to the Alamo for the first time, brought it all home. That Texan icon is not my own and will never be the icon of many people I know, but the fact the little mission still stands in the middle of busy, downtown San Antonio has something to do with playing Indian in school and with the 1992 celebration of the five hundredth anniversary of those three ships coming west.

The Alamo still stands as a Texan nationalistic altar, and will help the 1992 celebration of Columbus be successful, because many Americans got to build their own altars by playing cowboys and Indians on school grounds. Those of us who became writers because that inner silence burst upon our spirit, started writing for many undiscovered reasons. One of them has to be the childhood influence of being stuck on those monkey bars, yelling like the wild animals we were told we were. Even our skin was the right color to match our savage psyche, the appropriate madness to resist the deeds of Columbus or Cortés.

The year 1992 marks our survival on the losing side, a rare place to be for some Americans (except for Vietnam). The year 1992 means we came down off the monkey bars when the school bell rang and went to the next grade at the next school, our history texts never telling us not every American could run to the water fountain first, not all of us could be at the head of the line to please our teacher. And, we believed the whole thing until we graduated and had to look for work or try and find money to go to college.

The year 1992 is also significant because the history of the twentieth century demands the whole world stop and look back. The history of Western civilization shows that when a century turns, it is harder to overcome collective guilt, a convenient time to try to come to terms with our bloody ghosts. The problem with studying a five-hundred-year period is that there are too many lies, truths, deaths and conquests to ponder and analyze. There are too many school children dividing up into two sides. But, this time, we have more than twenty minutes of lunch hour left before the bell rings.

As a writer, I have been influenced by my shame in playing an Indian when I was a boy. To write and create is to rise above that playground level and get to class on time without having to wipe the dirt off my mouth. I have also been influenced by Steve Kinnard, Bruce Burns, John Dodson, and all the good guys who got to beat up on me, then take off their cowboy hats, and go into class without being counted tardy. Their books of poetry will win national prizes and get published because they wore the white hats. Their novels will make the best-seller lists and get reviewed in the *New York Times*. My writing is also haunted by the fifth-grade report I did on the *Niña, Pinta,* and *Santa María*.

I still want to sail to unknown lands and discover something, draw as innocently and precisely as I did in fifth grade, but that A+ paper dissolved into the earth a long time ago. As a poet, I keep digging it up out of that inner silence, but as I progress in my writing career, the cowboy hats keep popping up to remind me that Columbus influenced even the structure of American arts and letters.

As a Chicano writer, I have had to dangle from the monkey bars and come late to class because the *Niña, Pinta,* and *Santa María* have landed at harbors where Chicano, Native,

Black, and Asian American writers have not been allowed
to drop anchor. Greater opportunities may now be develop-
ing for so-called minority writers, and let's admit that 1992
has had a great deal to do with it. Yet, are they opportunities of only one year, a lifetime, or five hundred years?

If I can shake off that shame of being told I wasn't good
enough to be on the cowboy team, will I be able to write better poems, essays, or novels? Will more of my books get published? Will more East Coast publishers look at me because
they are tired of their guilt at having published and pro-
moted only the writers who made it to class on time? Are the
cowboy hats that Steve, Bruce, and John brought to school
now torn and frayed, or does 1992 mean that Columbus
shouldn't have gotten me an A+ on that report? Perhaps, I
only deserved a C because I couldn't tell the true story of
the conquest and genocide of the American continent.

How many of us grew up that way? I wish I had copies
of every textbook I was handed in my elementary school
years. One of my favorite tasks on the first day of school was
writing my name in neat, large script on the inside cover. It
meant a brand new year and fresh challenges for an intelli-
gent kid who knew that book was his and that he could de-
vour it in no time. I can imagine a close study of those books
would say a great deal about textbook adoption policies in
the state of Texas in the fifties and sixties, policies that have
not changed a great deal in thirty years.

Where is the historical truth? Why couldn't a boy like
me have the right to be taught the truth? Where is the
childhood part of me that is proud of that colorful drawing
of the *Niña, Pinta,* and *Santa María* I spent two weeks
working on?

Now, as a published writer, I know my history and I wait
for 1992 to run its course. I wait for other writers of my cul-

ture to be given an honest chance, but I also want to see how many writers are waving their childhood drawings of Columbus, or George Washington, or the Statue of Liberty. How many of them got to do fifth-grade reports on Benito Juárez, or Pancho Villa, or Augusto Sandino? How many of them have overcome their silence to respond to this American look at five hundred years of A+ reports?

In 1986, a National Endowment for the Humanities survey found that one-third of the nation's seventeen-year-olds did not know what year Columbus made his first voyage. Four percent of the students surveyed thought the voyage occurred after 1850. This says a great deal about our educational system, but also tells us that many people will not react to the media hoopla over 1992. Their world is still flat and, if they journey too far, they will fall off the edge.

Perhaps, the education I got as a child and the versions of history I based my A+ report on were better than I think. It might be more accurate to say the world has shrunk in five hundred years and Columbus' three ships started the shrinking. Today, CNN and MTV are the textbooks, not the old history readers I grew up with in the library.

It may be appropriate to celebrate Columbus and overdo it because of our sophisticated media environment. The technology may bring more views on the Columbus debate from scholars and historians in all parts of the globe. The electronic world is also responsible for those students not knowing when Columbus sailed and for the limited opportunities "minority" writers have.

Marking the five hundred years also means the American media and publishing industry have not needed to discover writers who drew pictures of the three ships thirty years ago, nor do they have a need for native writers who have been too aware of the real meaning of the year 1492.

Today's media audience does not need its own history. It may react to the celebration by defending Columbus as a true hero, and reject any notion that those who were exiled to the monkey bars have a history that says otherwise.

That may be an extreme way of looking at it, but Chicano writers have to revise history, preserve their own culture at the same time, and try to write good literature. All this must be done in the midst of a hot media environment that wants exciting stories for the five o'clock news, not essays about monkey bars and long-lost drawings of pretty ships.

Twelve full-scale replicas of the original ships have been built for the celebration. Spain's official three cost 4 million dollars. This is a small example of the 80 to 100 billion dollars estimated to be spent on 1992 events by several countries. These staggering sums include everything from the 50 million dollars worth of plants Columbus, Ohio, spends for "AmeriFlora '92," the nation's first international floral and garden exhibition, to the 10-million-dollar lighthouse the Dominican Republic builds in Santo Domingo.

Who knows how many ships will sail by that beacon, but that light may not reach far enough to blind several movements against the 1992 extravaganza. One of the most encouraging signs is the fact the United Nations General Assembly has not taken any official action to recognize the Quincentennial. Efforts to have it recognized have been stymied diplomatically. Iceland and Ireland claim their descendants invaded first. They want the honor. Several New World nations have fought all this, calling 1492 an "encounter," not a "discovery." So far, their resistance to a 1992 conquest has been successful.

In the middle of these far-reaching, sometimes ridiculous, at times heartening events, I keep thinking back to my

lunchtime games of cowboys and Indians and to my A+ report on the *Niña, Pinta,* and *Santa María.* History of my
childhood says my shame of being pushed off the monkey
bars, to get my face ground into the dirt by the tougher
cowboys was one of the strongest internal catalysts for becoming a writer. My history also says my talents as a student
were recognized for the report I gave on Columbus' three
ships, the way they were built, how they sailed, and how
many men they carried.

I recall the teacher pinned my drawing on the bulletin
board and kept it up there for several days. It hung alongside several other good reports, but it was the most colorful,
the most artistic. My history as a Chicano writer says I was
already waving the visions and colors of a dynamic, growing
literature before a tough audience, other kids who were
busy on their own voyages, drawing their own ships, hanging up their own hats, trying to write their own versions of
history, not knowing their fifth-grade dreams would someday be as important as every crucial political event that took
place between 1492 and 1992—crushing, monumental dra-
mas created across the continent of their lives.

The Active Poet

In the fall of 1970, I was a freshman English major at University of Texas, El Paso (UTEP) and enrolled in a contemporary poetry class taught by Robert Burlingame. Before the course, the only attention I had paid to poetry was when I was forced to read Shakespeare, Milton, or T. S. Eliot in high school. I suffered through their work and dismissed poetry as something impossible to understand.

One day in Dr. Burlingame's class, we were studying poems in the anthology *Naked Poetry* (Bobbs Merrill, 1969). I had never heard of most of the writers in the book, poets like Robert Lowell, James Wright, and William Stafford. We were discussing Stafford's poem, "Traveling Through the Dark," and Dr. Burlingame wrote a few lines from the poem on the blackboard. Stafford's words, "I thought hard for us all," stood out.

As Dr. Burlingame stepped away from the blackboard, I casually gazed at the lines he had written, and then read the whole poem to myself on the open page. All of a sudden, I saw poetry for the first time! There was no ray of light coming to strike me, but I felt different, and I knew that I was opening up to a poem. The puzzling process of reading poetry was melting away to be replaced by a clarity and understanding of a poem.

From that day on, I absorbed everything that I could in class and read more of Stafford, Wright, Robert Bly, and many others. Before long, I began writing poems myself, shifting from my imitation of rock-and-roll lyrics to more serious work. It would take years before I could call myself a poet and take my work seriously. But that day in Dr. Burlingame's class changed my life. I went on to enroll in the creative writing program at UTEP. I learned a great deal about poetry, and discovered that to write a good poem, I had to make a commitment to the *art of poetry.* Inspiration would never be enough and a magical moment with a poem like Stafford's would not carry me for the rest of my life. I had to *work* at poetry and develop craft, but I didn't know that in 1970.

Twenty-three years after Stafford's poem marked the beginning, I read poetry constantly. My various editing projects as a publisher of magazines and anthologies keep me in poetry all the time. I *need* it to be a successful writer and editor, and a director of a literature program. I read both good and bad poems, saying "yes" to myself when a poet has taken me into the poem, "no" when there is too much hidden. I thank Robert Burlingame for pointing me to poetry.

In addition to that magical day in Dr. Burlingame's class, there are several reasons why I became a poet. It has taken me this long to recognize the autobiographical factors. But if I discover all the motivational forces for being a poet, I would probably stop writing. Certain events transformed me into the person who could respond to the Stafford poem and go on from there. I stumbled through the dark, uncovering of the poetic process, writing terrible poems, coming up with a good one every now and then, silently surprised when I wrote very personal things as my poems took shape.

The solitude of a childhood in the desert influenced the

way I relate to the world. As a child, I had few friends and spent a lot of time alone in my grandmother's house in a barrio of El Paso. My childhood fantasies helped create the inner world of my poems. I built the inner circle of solitude at a very early age. I enjoyed spending time alone, talking to myself, creating characters in my head.

I was never athletic and was teased by the other boys. Being called "fatso" or "dumb Mexican" made me withdraw and reinforced my connection to a safer, inner existence. I wrote little stories in a notebook in grade school, mostly war stories and science-fiction. I wrote what I thought was a novel about the U.S. Cavalry invading Mexico. I was in the sixth grade. It filled one hundred handwritten pages. Of course I made the U.S. the good guys. I didn't know any better at the time.

As a teenager, I started writing song lyrics. This was around 1964–65. The early Beatles, the Rolling Stones, and Bob Dylan influenced my juvenile, corny lyrics. I still have several hundred of those lyrics tucked away somewhere. I began to respond to the world through the eyes of an introverted kid trying to make sense of it all, secretly writing in notebooks that I hid under the bed so that my mother would not find them and expose me to the rest of the world.

Perhaps I lived in fear of discovering my own creativity. There were voices and shadows of characters I made up in my head as I walked down the street near my grandmother's house. I talked to these invisible companions, although I could see them in my dreams and I placed them in the stories I wrote.

One of the strongest characters that influenced my need to write fell out of the sky one day. Every now and then, I dream about him and about the time I was caught in a furious lightning storm when I was five. I was playing down the street from my grandmother's house. I was alone when a sudden darkness filled the sky. I must have been too preoccupied in my fantasy world to notice the rain clouds overhead. The downpour was vicious and I bolted down the street. As I ran past neighbors' houses, lightning hit behind one of them. A globe of blinding light shot across the telephone wires. The noise deafened me for a moment and my ears rang. I was four or five houses away from home, drenched in a wall of water with lightning striking everywhere, when I saw a figure climb down one of the telephone poles. I thought he was a phone repairman, but what would he be doing up there with electricity firing around him?

Through the water and exploding bolts, I saw a figure clad in green. He looked like a lizard with slick, wet skin. His face was obscured by the rain and the lingering blindness of the flying light. I ran harder, then turned to see him jump off the pole and disappear behind a house. I made a dash across our porch and entered the house soaked to the skin. I never told anyone about the lizard man.

These experiences filled my first notebooks, which I kept hidden. What made me do that? Did an inner sense tell me that creativity cannot be developed in the open? Are the boundaries of American culture so ingrained in us that we naturally awaken to our creativity in secret? How could I allow myself a "sense of awe and gratitude" for my creativity when I was afraid to show it? These are the barriers writers must overcome as they develop. Sooner or later, we stumble into the realization that our creativity has to take us beyond natural human fear to writing. Gratitude comes as we grow older, as we accumulate notebooks and rejection slips, our acceptances before the small audience for poetry, boundaries set upon us at an early age that forced me to tuck my notebooks under my bed.

One of the places where I learned to respond was in the desert of west Texas and southern New Mexico. As poet Keith Wilson writes, to love the desert means that you are going to be marked for life, because the desert will not leave you alone and will always have a claim over you. I feel that the best poems I have written are those set in the Southwest—the magnetic power and stark beauty of the desert claimed me for years, made me wander the canyons and *arroyos,* climb the Franklin and Organ Mountains in search of a way to get closer to the native earth and the source of my work.

In order to write poetry from the heart, I had to confront the land where I grew up. I found an immense solitude among the cactus and rocks, and I discovered that the force of my poems rose from a mysterious connection to the desert. After years of exploring such a desolate area and walking through abandoned adobe ruins of past lives and towns, I came out a wiser poet and a wiser man.

Another desert poet, Richard Shelton, has discovered that when you walk in any direction, the star Vega, known to astronomers as "the falling vulture," will lead you straight into the desert. Living in the desert is a unique experience to write about, although writing about it brings out the universal experience of living anywhere. The desert makes one confront great landscapes in daily life, in one's mind and dreams, and in one's work. The magnetic force of the vast, empty canyons pulled me to write poems. Walking across the desert required discipline and coming to terms with the fear of isolation, perhaps a fear before gratitude.

In *Arctic Dreams* (Scribner's, 1986), Barry Lopez writes about how the vast landscapes of the Arctic North dominate the lives of the Eskimos. The native people respect the immense power of the ice and desolation, transforming their existence around it. Lopez sees the Arctic landscapes as living, breathing forms that are environmental and spiritual bloodstreams inside the Eskimo. I see the desert in the same way. Its vastness and my attempts to come to terms with it produced the need to write.

Writing poems about the desert can be stereotyped into "nature poetry." It has been in vogue, off and on, to write poetry about "getting back to nature." As Native American writers are more widely read, and as Chicano writers gain wider acceptance, there is the tendency to say they write about the same old thing. I have worried about writing nothing but "Southwest poetry."

The knowledge I have gained from the desert has shaped my poems, but it has also planted an intense restlessness inside me. I began to see that there was more to being a poet than solitude and vast fields of cactus and rock, the force that tied me to the land. I left graduate school at UTEP in 1978 and moved to Denver, where there were more professional opportunities for writers than in El Paso. When I left, I knew that in order to evolve as a poet, I would need to open myself to the world. Perhaps the artistic rewards would come later. I decided that the best way to do this was to leave the desert, share my poems, and show people that poetry is for everyone and does not belong under the bed. As a result, I moved from being a solitary poet to having a public career as a literary organizer, editor, and publisher.

Many poets complain that there are never enough opportunities to have their work noticed by the public. This is partly true because Americans generally believe that poetry is too difficult to understand. This was my own attitude before Dr. Burlingame's class. But instead of complaining about this anti-poetic attitude, I am committed to creating opportunities for poets and other writers to help widen the audience for their work.

Using poetry to communicate and as more than artistic self-expression led me into publishing. I became poetry editor of *The Bloomsbury Review* in March of 1982, after they published some of my poems and needed someone to choose poetry for the magazine on a regular basis. The magazine was only two years old and the original staff was taking shape. Ten years later, I am still selecting poetry for the magazine from the hundreds of manuscripts I get each month.

I became an editor for several reasons. The most important is to get poetry into print in a country that does not appreciate poetry. In the process, I have met many poets and have been lucky to be a part of the American poetry scene.

Stafford's poem on the blackboard woke me up. Burlingame's patience and wisdom woke me from my sleep. They were the catalysts for the introverted desert boy to step forward, not knowing that he would define the idea of an active poet based on what those two men did for him.

I want to live in the world as a poet whose place lies somewhere between the realities of living and the place where we find our eternal feelings. It is where we go to leave an infinite mark on the consciousness of poetry. As a poet and editor, what can I leave behind that will carry on, generation after generation, and is it possible? Or, is poetry a moment for "now," a spontaneous combustion from mixing my voice with the other person not caring if anyone discovers my words in the future?

My creativity was shaped at an early age. Years ago, I thought poetry was therapy against the realities of life—a lonely childhood, family problems, love relationships, and so on. I realize now that there is no such thing as *art as therapy*. Poetry comes from an active soul responding *to* the world—not running away from it. The kid listening to the radio will not turn it off and go to sleep. The professor writing on the blackboard will not go away. The manuscripts pouring into the editor's office will not stop flooding the mail. The desert will not shrink and disappear.

Someone asked me once whether I thought poets should be active and make things happen, or should they wait for something to occur and then write about it? A poet should do both. My active role is in writing, editing, and organizing poetry. My waiting side comes from the lingering influence of desert solitude. I do not know everything that I wait for as a poet.

Sometimes the poet must wait for things to happen, and doesn't always know which way to turn. It is the magic of poetry, never finding all the answers, but having to go sit under a cottonwood tree along the Rio Grande to recover things, to feel the mystery and gratitude through the poem.

This active process is seen by some poets as a quest for "otherness" in poetry and in everything we do as artists. For me, this search applies more to the solitary act of writing than to the public role of editor and publisher.

I have written poems about recurring dreams of a past life in the ancient pueblos. Through my poetic search to come to terms with those dreams, I come closer to understanding the past, present, and future beyond the moment when Stafford's words on the blackboard shattered a daydream. These recurring dreams take place in the desert with its canyons, cactus, and rocks pushing me to find the answers with each new poem. I am still drawn to the desert because I left something in my "other" life. As a poet in the world, I have a great deal of work to do—creative work as a writer, and as a publisher and anthologist. It is also to find the other person through my poems and the poems of others, to work to reaffirm the active power of poetry.

Road Kills

I drive away from the doctor's office, my arm aching with an injury from lifting weights. He says it is a shoulder impingement. I get into my car and enter my fourth week with a bad arm. I pull onto busy Northwest Military Highway and head south toward downtown San Antonio. This part of town is a newer suburb where the condos, office buildings, and shopping malls cut into the rich hill country, businesses sprouting around the thick wooded hills.

As I move down the road, trying to merge into the fast traffic, I see the dead deer on the left side of the highway. It is a huge buck with antlers pointing into the air like an unexpected sign of danger. I try to slow down to get a better look, but have to keep moving. I see blood on its long snout, huge legs bent under the dark brown body. Did a car hit it and the driver have the courtesy to move it off the road? Was it able to lie down and die in the yellow grass after it was hit?

I am startled by the sight of a dead deer in a heavily populated area. These suburbs rise in a recent wilderness, the city limits extending through the hill country without boundaries. There must be other deer nearby. As I pick up speed again, I wonder how often they get hit on this busy highway.

I have driven another hundred yards down the road when I see a red pick-up truck parked on the left shoulder.

A young man in cowboy hat and boots climbs out of the truck. I pass as he lifts the carcass of a large black dog off the road and tosses it in back of the truck.

I can't believe it. Two big, dead animals one hundred yards apart. Did the dog belong to the cowboy? I didn't see an official symbol on the truck. He didn't look like a city worker cleaning the streets. He may have been looking for his lost dog when he found it on the road.

What about the deer? Who will pick it up? Will anyone be tempted to take the horns? In this city, you never know. Is there a law against stealing road kills?

The radio has been playing in the middle of everything I have seen. As I encounter the scenes of animal carnage on the road, I hear comments on NPR about the fight between President Bush and Congress over a new crime bill. The Democrats are trying to pass the toughest crime laws they have supported. Bush says it isn't good enough because, some commentators claim, Democrats in Congress have caught him off guard by presenting a more conservative legislation than the Republicans are used to pushing. Passage of the bill, which would call for adding the death penalty to fifty more crimes, would give Bush a disadvantage in the election campaign of 1992.

I listen to the outrageous debate and think about the dead deer and the cowboy picking the dog off the road. What is happening here? Road kills have nothing to do with criminal legislation, yet the images of magnificent animals destroyed on busy streets make me connect the two issues.

Politicians are fighting over a crime bill that will not affect the madness of our society. Millions of animals are killed on city streets and highways every year. So what? Let's be concerned about gang wars, drive-by killings, drug problems, rape, and murder. Road kills are part of the scenic roads of America. People let their dogs and cats run free all the time. Cities grow and cars kill the rare deer that tries to cross the new pavements.

When I saw the deer by the side of the road, I was reminded that the things we do as individuals in a busy metropolis are insignificant—the jolting sight of the torn deer meaning nothing. When I spotted the huge antlers pointing to the sky, I expected to see somebody run up to the carcass and cut them off. It would have to happen in an instant. As I drove by, I imagined someone doing it, because it fit into the random killing of the animal. I don't know who cleaned it up or what became of it later, but I know the dead-animal truck from city sanitation keeps busy every day.

◆ ◆ ◆

One of the strangest sights I have ever seen appeared in 1971 on the dark freeway between El Paso and Las Cruces, New Mexico. A friend and I were driving to see the Allman Brothers Band in Las Cruces, back when we would go anywhere to catch a famous rock band perform a rare concert in New Mexico.

As we sped through the night, the long, straight miles of the interstate cut through the flat desert west of the Organ Mountains. Our headlights broke the blackness of the road and we saw the dying dog just in time to swerve around him. The dog looked like a coyote, but I wasn't sure. He had been hit just minutes before—and was still alive. As we drove by, the dog raised his head and front legs, but I could see that his back legs were crushed. The glare of our headlights ignited his unforgettable eyes for an instant. The black desert covered him again. We flashed by without a word.

Travelers spot dozens of road kills when they cross desert highways. The surprising image of the dog, still alive,

startled us because we were only used to seeing *flattened*
jackrabbits and dogs on the road. As we passed the struggling animal, there was something out in the blackness of
the desert I couldn't explain, a force that had made us witness the death throes of the dog.

The image of the half-crushed dog trying to rise from
the pavement comes back as I think about the deer. The radio says the crime bill is important, but the commentator
acknowledges that not enough Americans are going to pay
attention to the details. Chances are, Bush will get his way,
using a veto and Republican strategy to present his own
legislation, a move the public could care less about because
of their own immediate problems. Too often, like me, they
think about things other than the killing and maiming of
thousands of Americans each year, victims of their fellow
citizens in the most violent nation in the world.

A few years ago, I read that over three million dogs and
cats are killed on the streets of America yearly. In December, San Antonio records murder number 178 for 1991, a
high number, but city officials say it should not break the
1990 record of 219. The debate over the crime bill is gone
from the radio. Something happened in the legislative process. I do not know what was decided.

The murder rate rises in San Antonio, but I feel a sadness over the *deer*. Is there something wrong with this feeling? After our home was burglarized, my family and I fear
becoming victims of another crime. Dwelling on the deer
means I have the time to ponder other road kills, while I
also worry about runaway crime and madness in the country. As the Christmas season nears, the first anniversary of
the burglary approaches and I am apprehensive, checking
and rechecking the locks and bolts and alarm system we
installed after we were "hit."

As I check our safety, the image of the antlers and the scene of the cowboy tossing the dog into the truck come back. What am I looking for in those visions?

I remember a long-ago incident that took place during my first marriage (a traumatic failure that ended in divorce). My first wife and I were driving, late for a party at a friend's house because we had quarreled about something before leaving.

As I drove and she complained about our different ways of looking at things, I hit the gas and sped through a winding city street lined with trees. As we rounded a curve, I saw something small in the middle of the road. Thinking it was a dog or cat, I hit the brakes. It jolted us in our seats. We spotted the pigeon as it flew out of the way.

Even though we almost hit our heads on the windshield, she thought it was funny that I would brake to avoid hitting a bird. Everyone knows they are so fast, flocks of them move out of the way when cars approach. Her abrupt, mocking laughter shamed me. I had never braked for a pigeon before. I thought it had been a *bigger* animal. Our argument forgotten, she laughed all the way to our friend's house and proceeded to tell everyone about her husband who braked for birds! It was one of the last fights we had. We separated a few weeks later, not because of the pigeon, of course, but that strange kind of humiliation had helped put the icing on the cake. I had not thought about my silly reflex of braking for a bird in years. It had been the reaction of a careful yet angry driver, one who was going too fast around a curve, his wife yelling at him.

I list my memories of the dead deer and dog, the dying one in the New Mexico night, and the pigeon of divorce. They add up to a sense of loss—a shock of sudden death contributing to the power of insignificance in this country.

To most people, the random death of so many animals is as
unimportant as the debate over the new crime bill. Hundreds of cars whizzed passed the dead deer. How many
drivers registered what happened? Yes, there are more important things to worry about as you drive down a highway,
but I can't get over the feeling that there is more to this.
While road kills are not crucial moments in a frantic day,
they represent the fact that violent deaths of crime victims
can be as easily dismissed as the death of so many animals.
In the U.S., the high crime rate and the uncontrollable gang
problem is our version of road kills. These street, school,
and city deaths are not being taken seriously by enough
people. They have become as insignificant as hitting a dog
or cat on the road. People don't notice unless it happens to
them or someone near to them.

◆ ◆ ◆

As I drive away from the deer and dog, the radio commentator thanks the politicians for debating the crime bill.
It does not become a campaign issue because they find a
way to soften the debate. I enter the busy streets of downtown San Antonio and forget about the radio program because I am stuck in traffic. Two black mongrels dodge cars
near Market Square, the busy tourist shops near where I
work. When the light turns green, cars honk their horns to
get the dogs out of the way. The dogs disappear through the
courtyard of the shops.

I reach the parking lot of the arts center where I work
and cross the street to the office building. The familiar
empty bottles of beer lie on the bus bench near the door, a
sight that greets me daily. I immediately spot the blood
splattered on the sidewalk.

Inside the office, the receptionist and the custodian are

talking about the drunks, two young Chicano men who had wandered into an event at the Guadalupe Theater. Someone called an ambulance when they saw that one of the drunks had a slashed throat. The drunk had wandered across the street toward the office, screaming for help. I don't catch the whole story, but he survived. I also hear the custodian's complaints about hosing off the sidewalk. His voice disappears as he goes to hook up the hose to wash the blood away before the director of the center arrives.

As I sit at my desk, I wonder who will get to the deer first. I hope the cowboy in the red truck will find some solace if the dog was his. At least he knows what it is all about. As for the question of why I didn't do something about the deer myself, I have no answer. Those bloodstains outside the door dictate my concerns about the safety of working in a violent city that keeps growing and spreading beyond the familiar streets of death.

PART THREE

Mama Mescal

El *Guzano Rojo!* The red worm that soaks in the bottle of mescal. Mama Mescal! The oily drink for a July sunset along the Rio Grande, sitting on the porch of my house a hundred yards from Mexico. Mama Mescal! The oil that burns down the throat and makes your head dance, makes you see a "vision" that is truly a vision. Drinking this poison, mightier than tequila, is the search for power that often eludes you as you wander the desert and *arroyos.*

Swallow the shot of mescal, lick the salt off your hand, bite the sweet lime and watch the sky turn orange with the evening and the cottonwoods sway along the river as you sway along the porch. Mama Mescal! Dark brown, oval glass bottle we smuggled back from *el mercado* in Juarez, bought for two dollars to drink with cold limes. Gary and Jeff, my poet friends, step into this border life for the first time, reminding me of two children invading their father's liquor cabinet.

Mama Mescal! Why does the head want to float and glide as you walk and why does the grass along the canal wave without a wind? Why does the July night darken so quickly? Mama Mescal calls you to get recklessly drunk, something you rarely do. Each shot glass is full of yellow liquid bringing you closer to home, closer to the hour of vision when you see what you are meant to see. You pass the bottle and try to read poems aloud at the same time.

"Here is 'Ode to the Socks' by Neruda!" we cry, but
can't read the poem because Jeff and Gary keep asking if it
is true that you hallucinate if you drink too much mescal. I
laugh and bite the lime. A candle burns on the small table
we set out on the porch. The flame creates a dim circle of
light flickering over our grinning faces. What do we celebrate? That it might rain when it hasn't rained for weeks
and July is a hot month? The grove of cottonwoods in the
yard is full of sleeping sparrows, the high grass hides chirping crickets. The sound of a distant train whistle brings us
back to the fact that the bottle is half-empty and the worm
still floats on the bottom, waiting for the brave man among
us who will take his turn pouring his shot. By sacred fate,
the worm will drop into his glass, the sign that he is the chosen one for the night.

Mama Mescal! Our poems stumble on our tongues as
we try to recite them. "Here is 'Song of the Pissing Multi-
tudes' by Federico García Lorca!" We can't even read it because we rise to take a piss in the yard. The earth moves as
we move. A cool breeze shakes the trees. We hear voices of
merriment across the river. We are hungry for the moment
of vision absent in our poems, the opening of the night into a splendid aura delivered by the proud passing of the
bottle—the beauty of hitting the shot, licking the salt off
the hand, and biting the lime.

Eyes half-closed and my head spins with the candle
flame. My friends speak about poetry and life along the river, watch Mexico and wonder what it gives and takes from
its people, what we steal from the life of poverty to deny the
starving Mexicans in their cardboard shacks across the
river. A bunch of drunk liberals, we don't have any answers.

Mama Mescal! It calls me. Ringing ears because Mama
Mescal calls me. I am the chosen one because I tilt the bot-

tle y el guzano rojo drops into my glass! Mama Mescal! The night buzzes when I raise the glass to my lips, hands shaking with anticipation, a few drops spilling out of the glass. The worm sparkles in a yellow mist. I stop, put the glass down and sprinkle salt between my thumb and forefinger. Gary and Jeff laugh and wait jealously for me to swallow the worm, the visionary prize we have drunk for all night.

Gulp down the shot and worm, lick the salt, close the eyes and bite the lime. I suck the juices until my lips burn. I throw the glass down on the table and grin at my friends. Mama Mescal! Mama Mescal! I stumble into the dark yard as everything flashes into blue and purple lights. I hear them yelling at me. I wave to them and they run after me. I weave along the canal, shake off their attempts to pull me back from the water's edge. "It's the poem!" I cry. "It's the poem!" They guide me back to the porch. I cut loose from their grasp and run under the trees until they grab me again, walk me around the yard, holding me under each arm, keeping me on my feet and breathing.

Mama Mescal! Holy visions! July night in El Paso del Norte. The worm and the candle! The Rio Grande churns under the boiling stars. My words and the sudden black explosion in my head . . .

Mama Mescal. I open my eyes in the painful sunlight of the next morning. My face is pasted in vomit to the bed, my naked body spread like a drying worm, my head hammering. Gary and Jeff smile in the doorway of the stinking bedroom.

"Mama Mescal!" They laugh. "A vision!" they scream and point to me.

Mama Menudo

The mescal night inspires you to get up on an early Sunday morning, hot Texas sun shining, making you crazier than the hangover your brain kisses. You hear yourself gasp, *"¡Menudo! ¡Mama Menudo!"* You must go to La Paloma Café and wave your pained face over a big steaming bowl of hot, quivering chunks of menudo. It is an emergency. Your soul calls for it, prays to it, waits for the red spirit of the Menudo God to bless you and save you from the big mescal death.

You know menudo is the greatest thing anyone has ever sunk his teeth into. Nothing else comes close. Nothing else forces you to get into your car to drive a couple of miles down Paisano Street on a day when everyone else is in church praying. They listen to the Padre whose church sells menudo in the dining hall after *la misa. Los señores y señoras, sus hijos, los vatos*—they all pray first before thinking of eating menudo.

Not you. Your stomach moves like a dying river, a settling of flowing juices needing fresh slices of cow tripe to rise again and be reborn, putting life back into your existence, the magical source of survival in the desert.

Paisano Street is a wide, empty road of newspapers, trash, old tires, and dust. It is nearly empty of traffic, a Sunday morning in south El Paso looking like an abandoned movie lot, cardboard buildings warping in the heat, the parking lot behind La Paloma stinking of dog shit, half a dozen empty bottles of Carta Blanca reminding you of last night, the mescal and the limes.

You enter La Paloma because Mama Menudo is waiting, the sweet smell of a Mexican restaurant dampening your head. You are glad to see the place is nearly empty. The only other customer is an old Mexican sitting heavily at the counter, his huge body pressing into the stool, a bright cloud of steam rising from the bowl of menudo he hugs with thick hands.

You don't care that your favorite booth has a new tear in the old vinyl seat. None of the springs have popped through yet. It is the right place to sit.

Sylvia, the young waitress, knows what you want. She spots the menudo gleam in your red eyes and smiles beautifully at you. *"¿Café y un plato de menudo?"*

"Si, por favor." You smile back, the smell of sizzling chorizo and fresh tortillas sprinkling through your nose, preparing you for the taking of the holy food, a transcendence you have tried to describe to your friends—a state of menudo mind you share with your family, and with only a few converted friends.

Sylvia takes your order and you wait, this period very important, a silent oath of patience calming your heart to ease the hangover. The old man is hunched over his bowl. John F. Kennedy smiles at you from his portrait above the door. The painting of a pigeon, *la paloma*, reflects over the long mirror that stretches the length of the café.

Sylvia brings the silverware and the revolving cup holder, each container holding the magic ingredients that are part of the ceremony. You look into the cup of freshly cut onion, glad to see it is as full as the cups of oregano, chili piquin, and lemon slices. You set it on the right side of the table, the place it must always be. As you spread your arms over the table, Sylvia comes out on cue with the smoking bowl of menudo.

You hear the bells of the church ring down the street as she sets the offering before you. *"Gracias."* She leaves the bowl to steam into your eyes, knows you must eat alone, and quickly pours the coffee. You wait for her to leave.

The ritual begins. Two spoons of oregano flake into the bowl. The menudo is finely cut this morning, thin square strips floating among the *posole.* The soup is a dark red. You know it is a message from Mama that this mixture comes from a hot chili. Two spoons of chili piquin follow spoons of onion bits. The thing looks like a collage of chili, meat fat, jello, and black and green grains that emerge from the oregano. An innocent, ignorant person would say it looks like dog vomit and leftover cooking grease! But you love it and that person will never know the meaning of life, never understand why eating Mama Menudo is wild ecstasy and greedy pleasure—and most of all—it saves your life!

You slurp it like an anteater slurps ants, like a vacuum cleaner slurps dirt, like a monkey eats a banana, like a man slurps himself into sleep to wake up in search of his mama. Your right hand boasts of great skill. It digs spoonfuls of menudo straight into your mouth. The stuff is hot. You sigh as the chunks burn your tongue on their way down your throat. It does not take long. It never can. No one takes his time eating menudo. It is a creation of consumption, a snortling and grinding of the senses. The chili makes your eyes water, your ears pop, and it magically takes away the hangover. Your pupils blossom awake. Your heart beats proudly into the world. Your stomach flips awake like a dog that spots a cat and sprints for it!

It vanishes in a final gulp. A thin film of red grease that looks like blood glitters over the inside of the empty bowl.

You touched the coffee only twice. You came up for air once. Your nose runs. You are safe and happy. Something moves inside you. You sit still for a few moments, arms resting quietly on the table. A huge burp tries to leap out of you. You hiss it through your teeth. Sylvia appears a final time to see that everything has fallen into place. At the cash register, you pay the dollar fifty. As she counts the change, you pull your pants higher at the waist and see the old man waddle toward you, his ancient body having accepted grace from Mama Menudo as boldly as you have.

Sylvia gives you the change. As you tip her, the old man stands behind you to pay. You turn to say *"Buenos dias,"* and your eyes are filled with the color he wears on his gray shirt, the red badge of courage. A couple of menudo stains shine on his chest and chin.

"Yes," you cry in your heart, "this man knows." He is one of Mama Menudo's lost sons who has returned. You wait in the morning sun for the old man to step out of La Paloma. Standing by your car, you watch him move slowly down the sidewalk. He pauses at the corner, turns around to face you. He raises his right arm slowly and points a friendly finger at you. He smiles and crosses the street as you climb into your car. Before starting the engine, you look down at your T-shirt. It is a clean white, not a single drop on it. You look at the doorway of La Paloma and something moves in your stomach, tells you to come back to reclaim the red badge of menudo stain and wear it on your chest.

Christmas Tamales

Years ago, my friend Bill and I ate twenty-six tamales during one Christmas meal. He had fourteen, and I devoured a personal record of twelve. The tamales were made by my mother, Beatrice. That we could eat that many tamales in one sitting is not really amazing, because that kind of gluttonous ecstasy can be very common every Christmas among lovers—of tamales.

My mother makes the best tamales in El Paso and the dozens she produces during the Christmas holidays are part of an old Mexican tradition of having tamales for the holidays. The steaming *masa* pies, full of delicious pork and red-hot chile, roll out of the *hojas,* or corn husks, like little bundles of joy.

I can't recall a Christmas without tamales, but was astounded at the record my mother and sisters set in one December, when they hand-made sixty pounds of tamales, or thirty dozen of them. That equals three hundred and sixty tamales that Bill and I could have wiped out in a matter of days, back when we set our record. It took weeks for the whole family to enjoy them.

Making that many tamales at home is hard work. It took my mother and sisters two days to accomplish the feat. I wish I had been there to see the preparation, even though I was there to consume my share of the results. (Bill and I can never break our record. Middle-age brings larger tamale bellies on the outside, but smaller stomachs on the inside.)

Most tamale lovers don't know the steps involved in making them. They just like to peel the hojas off and eat them. When I helped out, I learned about the art of tamale cooking and have wanted to try it again, because the tasty results come from a very earthy, hands-on process. I believe the unique flavor of tamales is enhanced by the fact that you use your bare hands and fingers all the way from creation to consumption. The toiling palms of the tamale maker add a natural spice to them. Even with clean hands, of course.

The most important ingredient is the masa, or maize. Finding good corn flour in El Paso is not that easy. The texture of the masa has to be just right or the tamales will not cook to perfection. Most people would go to a Safeway and buy the masa prepackaged, like regular flour, but in El Paso, the key to good tamales is buying masa from a *tiendita,* usually a run-down grocery store in the barrio of El Paso.

I took my Aunt Consuelo to buy masa. The tiendita was no larger than a city bus and was located off Copia Street in the central part of town. When we entered the little shop, I immediately smelled the musky, overpowering scent of the masa. The woman behind the counter took our order of several pounds and turned to run the masa through the corn meal grinder, called a *molino.*

The masa comes in a thick, heavy paste made from ground meal and water. Running it through the molino grinds it down further and rolls it out in big chunks that look like wet cement, or mud pies. The woman packed the masa in butcher paper. Buying it this way is not cheap. We paid twenty dollars for several pounds, but we got the best.

According to my mother, corn meal spoils if it is not refrigerated and used right away. Warm masa can bring food poisoning the same way a badly prepared turkey can. After I brought the masa home, she wasted no time in cooling it, then dumping it into the *tina,* a large metal tub where the hand ritual takes place.

After salt, melted lard, and baking powder are added to it, the masa must be kneaded and pounded into the right texture. I got this job, which turned out to be my favorite part of making tamales. I stood before the huge tub of thick, gooey stuff and sunk my hands into it. It felt like grainy sand. My job was to knead the hard balls of masa into a smooth texture that could be spread on the husks with a spoon, one tamale at a time. It felt like I was giving someone a back massage. I put all my weight into it and kneaded and kneaded, grabbed and pinched and squeezed. As my fingers sank into the masa, I uncovered ball after ball of unkneaded dough. I had to find them all and churn the whole thing until it reached a fine fluffiness, the sign that the masa is ready for the slowest, most tedious task of all—painting corn husks with the white stuff. I kneaded for over half an hour to get the masa into form.

The final test to see if the masa is ready comes from an old folk tradition of cooking tamales, generation after generation. My mother took a glass of water, dipped a spoon into the masa, then dropped the tiny ball into the glass. The masa ball floated to the top. She nodded and told me that a floating masa ball means it is ready for the hojas. If the masa had sunk to the bottom of the glass, I would have to knead some more.

The hojas are odd, dried leaves that have served man for centuries. Indians had many uses for them as the tamale evolved from a native food to a Mexican delicacy. The husks are sold in bundles and are very cheap and usually available in grocery stores, but in our monumental year, there was a corn husk crisis that resulted in a shortage of commercial tamales. Many tortilla factories and tamale take-out cafés throughout the Southwest couldn't sell their usual tonnage of tamales. Mexican importers of corn husks were hit with spoiled, diseased leaves. U.S. Customs kept many husk suppliers from bringing husks into the country because a corn parasite devastated many corn crops in Mexico that year. Earlier, it hadn't been a problem and my mother was lucky to find enough husks for the record production two years later. I wonder how many tamale lovers had to settle for Christmas menudo when a little worm spoiled the holiday tamales.

Spreading the masa onto the husks takes hours. It is a messy job, similar to working with Play-Doh or plaster of paris. The kitchen table is cleared, then covered with newspapers to collect the dripping masa. My sisters and I sat around a table, grabbed a stack of husks, and began to cover them. This involves dipping a spoon into the tub and spreading the masa evenly onto the open husk. You hold a husk in your left hand and spread with your right.

After two spoonfuls of masa cover each husk, another person takes the prepared ones and spreads a large spoonful of red chili onto the masa surface. The red chili is cooked with thick cubes of pork in giant vats. It can be mild, hot, or outrageous. The best tamale chile is made from the long, dried chili peppers that can be bought in bags at most grocery stores. Once the stems and seeds are removed, the remaining peppers are placed in boiling water and left to sit. After they have soaked, the chilies are thrown into a blender and mixed with water. The blended chilies come out in a thick paste because the skins still need to be removed. This means running the sauce through a sieve and spooning the pure chili into bowls. The skins left in the sieve are thrown away. The hot stuff is cooked with the pork to produce the best tamale chili. Plenty of cumin seed gives it a special flavor.

After the husks are filled with masa and chili, each tamale is carefully folded so none of the ingredients fall out while they are being cooked. The final step is steaming the tamales for an hour and a half. They are placed, a couple of dozen at a time, in a pressure cooker. The tamales can be stacked around a wire basket holder, similar to those used for steaming canning jars. My mother claims it is important that the same person who sets the tamales into the steamer be the one to watch them and take them out when they are done. If anyone interferes with another person's batch, the tamales will not come out right.

The results of good cooking is an unforgettable Christmas feast. I could have eaten a dozen tamales in one sitting during that visit, but it would have been disastrous. Tamales are delicious, but the weight of the masa can be felt in your body for days. Yet it is a small price to pay for sharing in a special, family tradition. Eating tamales gives us a sense of sharing, enhanced by the home-made creation. As Bill said many years ago, after swallowing fourteen tamales, "These things are great!"

PART FOUR

The Blue Room

The most disturbing experience of growing up in my grandmother's house in the central barrio of El Paso was the blue room—the playroom my parents set up for me as the firstborn.

The blue room was in the back of the house, to the right of the back porch, another area of mystery to me. My parents wall-papered the room in blue designs that I can no longer recall because in my memory the walls vibrate with a darkening light that keeps those details from me. From then on, the whole family referred to it as "the blue room." One of the first television sets in El Paso could be found in the blue room, along with my playpen, high chair, crib, and dozens of toys—a kingdom for a spoiled first child.

The blue room becomes a glowing cavern. I am three years old. I am walking in the crooked, fragile way of a toddler, crossing the blue room toward my parents' bedroom. I trip on the doorstep, the low ridge of wood on the floor between the rooms.

I fall down and pass out, to the horror of my grandmother. She picks me up and revives me. How, I don't recall, but I see the blue walls spinning above me as she holds me in her arms, wondering what has happened. My parents are called on the phone and told. When they come home from work, they take me to the doctor. He finds nothing wrong.

I play in the blue room every day, my favorite toy truck

127

and tractor rolling across the wooden floor, the tiny, wooden horse rocking by itself whenever I tag its skis. I push the truck toward my parents' room. It bounces over the doorstep, crashes across the floor. I instinctively reach out to catch it, tumble to the floor, and pass out.

A second visit to the doctor and nothing is wrong with me. My grandmother watches me closely. I am held prisoner in the blue room, the glow from the small TV screen rising in the late afternoon heat, the curtains closed to keep out the heat. *The Mickey Mouse Club* comes on with its familiar opening song. In my excitement, I run in front of the TV, fall before my grandmother, and faint again, two days after the previous occurrence.

Medical tests show I am anemic. Any sudden physical action, like a careless landing on the floor, will cause these fainting spells. The doctor claims I am not well, even though I eat the wonderful bowls of beans and tortillas that my grandmother often cooks. (Perhaps poverty in our family kept good nutrition away, my parents working hard, my grandmother doing the best she could to raise me.)

The blue room expands in my sleepy head. I am lying in my crib, trying to take a nap in the middle of the day, my grandmother laying me down after one of those fainting spells, the sixth one in two months. The walls of the blue room are like ocean water I have never seen. I swim through it in my dreams, a boy wondering what is going on, why the sudden spark of light comes shooting through the distant TV screen to cover the Mouseketeers, to disrupt their songs as I plunge into darkness.

I lie there as the sun starts to go down. My parents are not home. I am afraid and the house is quiet, the heat mixing with the blue haze in the room, my grandmother napping in her bedroom. The TV is silent. My bottle lies nearby, but I don't want it because I am lost in a blue dream of doorways, toy trucks, songs, and laughter. The emptiness of an abandoned house rocks in its silence, forcing a child to huddle deeper into his blue walls of protection, the room with toys always there when he wakes from the darkness.

The last memory of the blue room comes a few years after I have stopped fainting, no longer anemic but now headed toward long years of obesity and the constant putdowns by school kids for being fat. We are moving to our new home, and my grandmother's house is empty, the movers having taken away the furniture. I wander through the house, amazed at the echoes I pick up in the empty rooms. I go to the blue room and stare at the fading wallpaper. My legs begin to shake as I stand in the doorway with the sensation of falling into darkness in this hour of abandonment.

It is early evening. I am three years old again. I can't find my parents. They are working or visiting friends. I can't find my grandmother. She is not in her room or in the kitchen where she spends most of her time baking tortillas. *The Mickey Mouse Club* comes on. The glare of the TV screen erupts with a pop. I am sitting in my little rocking chair in front of the screen. As the TV comes on by itself, I am frightened and leap out of the chair. I run to find my grandmother, although I know I am the only one in the house. I trip on the doorstep, the raised wood like a wall of control holding me back, but tossing me through the air. I go tumbling, my shoes untied, my legs doing a perfect trip as I slide across the wooden floor, cry like the child I am, and then faint.

The blue room moves toward me, the walls covering me in warmth. The glow of the TV forms a tiny ball of light behind me. I roll slowly onto my back, catch the last images on the screen. I fall gently into the safety of sleep, where the

internal presence of light and air welcomes me, until panicked arms hook me back into the real world. The arms let
go, my signal of freedom to run out of the empty house. I
move fast, eager to say good-bye to the neighborhood of old
adobes, good-bye to the color of blue, to the shade of wall
opening in my searching sleep.

Tío José

My drunk uncle causes trouble—again. Tío José comes home at seven in the morning, ranting and pounding on the back door of Doña Julia's house, my grandmother. Tío José is drunk and she won't let him in. He has done this too many times. I get up from bed when I hear him scream, *"¡Vieja puta!"* I look out the window as Tío José stumbles across the yard and falls into the patch of *nopales,* the cluster of prickly-pear cactus in Doña Julia's garden. Tío José falls face first into the thorns and lies still in the morning sun.

Doña Julia comes out the back door and rushes to the still body of her drunk brother. The old woman, dressed in a faded yellow dress and black shawl, turns on the garden hose full blast and sprays Tío José. He doesn't move, but lies motionless with his arms pinned in the thick plot of nopales, his head buried between two giant cactus.

She waters the garden with the *borracio* in the middle of her nopales. I watch her turn off the water and go back inside. I stare at the frozen body of Tío José until I see him move a leg, then an arm. He rises slowly to his knees. His torn T-shirt is caked with mud. His faded khaki pants are stained with blood from his swollen arms.

I step back when I see him stumble in the wet garden. I look in time to see him fall into the cactus again. I turn away when I see Tío José's face has landed against one of the biggest cactus. I hear the panting and low screams of the borracio and know I will never eat another bowl of Doña Julia's nopales from the garden.

Thirty-four years later, I can't get rid of the image of Tío José lying crucified to the prickly-pears, a drunk at the center of two of my earliest memories. I must have been two when I remember him holding me in his arms as my mother took our photograph in front of the house. He wore a white T-shirt then, too, the tattoos on his arms bulging at the child staring at him.

The second memory is of the drunk in the thorns who vanished from the face of the earth when I was six. The last my family heard, he was somewhere in Los Angeles, calling my mother from jail, in 1958. He has been missing ever since. No one knows what happened to Tío José, the man in my earliest memory fever. He was the drunk who showed me how close my family was to the bitter sharpness of the earth—nopales to grow, harvest, and consume in my grandmother's garden, their rich, vegetable aroma drifting above the crucified man in their arms.

My Father's Pool Hall, 1964

Sunland Billiards was the first commercial pool hall granted an operating license by the city of El Paso. My father opened it in the spring of 1964. There were great expectations in the family because it was his first business. When it opened, it was the only billiard parlor in town. I was twelve years old and didn't know anything about the business, but learned a great deal about shooting pool. I also saw a short-lived dream of success turn into disillusionment, financial ruin, and the start of long years of family poverty.

At the time, I enjoyed the fact that my father was the boss of a place I could get into for free, a benefit few boys had. Plus I could get free Cokes, peanuts, and beef jerky while I played endless games of eight-ball. When I wasn't trying to sink the balls without scratching the cue ball into the pocket, I could sit in red vinyl booths in the lounge and watch the customers drink beer at the bar and act like crazy adults.

Their laughter and cigarette smoke spread beyond the small lounge into the huge room full of billiard tables. Bored with their drunk speech, a mixture of Spanish and English, I would run into the main room and count all the tables. There were sixteen of them, two without pockets for the traditional game of billiards. I loved to walk down the rows of tables and click the dials that kept the scores. I enjoyed grabbing as many chalk cubes as I could find to rub

133

them into the tips of the cue sticks. Finding a brand-new cube of blue chalk was a thrill. The new ones squeaked the loudest when I ground them into the stick.

I learned to play by watching all types of men come to Sunland, bend over the tables, aim, and jab their sticks at the freshly racked balls. The loud snap of the cue ball breaking the triangle of color became a familiar sound that I loved to imitate with a snap and pop of my mouth. The players who caught my attention the most were the *caballeros* from Juarez and the G.I.s from Fort Bliss, two different kinds of men with pool savvy.

The Mexican men were cool and slick. They showed a smooth, professional way of playing. I thought billiards was only a U.S. sport, but these men from across the border were the best shots, the best drinkers, and had the most attractive women with them.

At the age of twelve, I was just starting to notice the women. I was too young to pick out the prostitutes from the women who hung out at Sunland. I recall tight dresses and long legs as they sparkled under the dim red and blue lanterns revolving on the lounge ceiling. I would stare at these women as they kissed and hugged the men, wondering if parents ever did that in public.

The most vivid image of women who were drawn to pool halls came from Esperanza, the girlfriend of Sammy, one of my father's employees. I never paid much attention to her, until the day I walked past one of the booths where Sammy sat with another Mexican man. They were drinking and laughing, passing something between them. Out of curiosity, I stopped at their table and got a quick look at a photo of a naked Esperanza. Her huge breasts jumped out at me. I hurried past the table. They never looked up.

This was in contrast to the G.I.s who came to Sunland

and gave it most of its business. The soldiers had fun there without women. They would show up in groups of three or four, young crew-cut boys from around the country who may have been amazed that there was only one pool hall in town. Once they found it, they became regulars on weekends, filling most of the tables for a few loud games before going on to their next destination. Many times, I heard them talking about the whorehouses in Juarez.

One of the most exciting games I witnessed was between two G.I.s—a tall black man and a muscular white guy. They were buddies, but very competitive. Their intense game of eight-ball drew a crowd. I managed to squeeze through the other G.I.s to get a good look. The black guy sank six in a row before missing. The other soldier made one ball that set up a tricky shot. He twisted over the table and held the stick vertically to make sure the cue ball would jump and hit the right ball.

The white ball missed everything and bounced off the table with a loud bang. It flew past me. I chased it under the next table. When I got up to give it to him, I saw the look of impatience bordering on hatred in his eyes.

"Gimme dat," he hissed in a Southern drawl.

I handed the ball to him. He snatched it away. His triumphant buddy pocketed several dollars off the table. I stopped watching and went to sit in the lounge.

I did not go to the pool hall every day, only when my mother drove down Montana Street to help out, or when I went with my father on weekends. The bar business bored me, although my attraction to the game increased. I always played alone and chose empty tables away from the customers. If any of them wanted my table, I had to give it up. I would have refused if any of the men had asked me to play. None of them ever did because they were on the clock. It cost 60 cents an hour to play. Every customer had to punch in at the counter before being handed a set of balls. In 1964, a penny a minute was a lot of money.

Playing alone meant I had the freedom to practice, improve my game, make up my own rules. Most pool players I knew held the stick in the professional way of the shooting arm and stick over the other hand, flat on the table to allow the stick to glide smoothly between the thumb and forefinger. I had my own style of holding the stick and running it over my other hand. It was a manner only a young kid could come up with, as he imagined himself to be a great pool shark.

It took months of shooting to learn the angles and tricks of sinking the balls. The hardest part was putting enough power behind my arm when breaking the tight triangle of balls. I could not get any of the balls to fall into the pockets on a break. I never played a game of pool with anyone else during the days of Sunland Billiards. I became a better pool player in high school and college when I had friends to play with, years after the Sunland days were over.

I spent hours shooting pool while my father tried to make his business successful. He never said much to me about the pool hall, so I don't know how he felt about being a businessman. He said even less when business started slowing down. This silence between us drove me further into my solitary games of eight-ball. I can still see my father standing behind the bar, laughing with the customers as the first suds of beer pour out of a freshly tapped keg and spout. He seems happy behind the bar. He is in charge, the business is new, and he is dreaming of success.

The only time anyone tried to shoot pool with me was in the summer of 1965, near the end of Sunland Billiards. It was a quiet Saturday afternoon, with two or three people at the bar and an old Mexican man at one of the tables. As I lined up the balls on my table, I could hear my parents arguing in the other room, disagreements over why business had gone so bad, why the bills weren't being paid, why so little money was coming in.

The old man put on a great exhibition of pool for himself and me, the only ones there. It was thrilling to witness his skill at playing the odd traditional game of billiards— only three balls on the table and no pockets. Most customers stayed away from the difficult game, preferring the tables with pockets, not even knowing how to play billiards. I watched him coolly calculate the angles he needed to make sure the balls ricocheted off each other. He wore a sweat-stained cowboy hat, a faded Levi's jacket, and a huge pair of muddy black boots.

He knew I was watching him and would glance over to grin at me before making a difficult shot. He walked to my table when I broke the balls with a loud whack. None of them dropped in.

"Play eight-ball?" he asked me in a squeaky, heavily accented voice.

I nodded, not sure what to say to my first challenge ever. He grinned, muttered something in Spanish and began to knock the striped balls into their pockets. He seemed to miss on purpose to give me a chance. I was very self-conscious, but managed to sink three balls in a row before my mother hurried into the room, motioning that we were leaving.

"Adios, muchacho," the old man said to me. He handed me his worn chalk cube and went back to his game. I looked down at the crumbling blue chalk as if given a gift. I put it in my pocket as my mother hurried me out of Sunland.

I was shocked at the anger and pain on her face. Things

were not going well. Sunland Billiards had been in business for one year. During that time, my father had worked hard to make it go, but the city had started licensing more pool halls and the competition increased. The novelty of the first pool hall in town faded quickly. The final blow was not being able to pay taxes to the city as the profits went down.

The last attempt to save the place was to turn it into a dance hall. The tables were slowly sold to other pool halls and the huge room became a dance floor. My father hired musicians to play, but hardly anyone came to dance. By August of 1965, the place was closed.

Long after the last pool tables stored in our garage had been sold, I was exploring piles of boxes and junk stored there. I was trying to build a tree house with my neighborhood friends. I gathered wood and nails from the shelves. As I pulled boards and boxes, a large cardboard drawer came apart under the wood. I yanked on the carton and dozens of white index cards spilled onto the cement floor.

I bent down to find they were the time cards from Sunland Billiards. The box was full of them. Each had been punched with the purple ink from the time clock to keep track of how much each table owed. I shuffled through dozens of them and thought back to the fun days at the pool hall, the endless games I played without having to punch in or out. I wished we had kept one of the tables in the garage, but my father needed to sell them all to make ends meet. I dug deeper into the carton and found a couple of chalk cubes, both of them worn down by the sharks anxious for the next shot.

I saved one of those time cards after my parents got rid of the last evidence of a failed business. By 1966, my father was struggling as a used-car salesman, barely bringing home enough money to buy groceries. I didn't know it then, but

I believe now that the pool hall was a turning point in my parents' marriage. After the business failed, they worked hard to pay off the debt, the loans, struggling to put food on the table for me and my three sisters. For years after, I watched my father work at sleazy used-car lots and saw my mother wait up for him to come home, so she could feed him a late-night dinner. It was the beginning of the end, a crumbling that took almost another twenty years to complete in divorce.

I no longer shoot pool and have lost the touch. The few times I drove by the corner of Montana and Pershing Streets, I stared at the empty lot. The building was torn down years ago. The last time I drove by, the unexpected image of my father laughing behind the bar came to me. He looked happy with an air of freedom about him.

As I turned the corner onto Montana Street, those time cards came flying back to me. I saw them pile up behind the counter, and I wanted to jump up there to ask my father if I could punch the clock. He let me because time meant money when you owned the newest, largest pool hall in El Paso. The clicking of the billiard balls increased the ticking sound on the timer that kept track of those pennies that rolled in by the minute.

Rocking Out at Woolworth's

I discovered rock-and-roll on the radio in 1964. I listened to Top 40 hits on station KELP. My first radio was a tiny, plastic gray one my parents passed on to me after the case broke. It was electric and had great sound despite the fact that I held the back panel on with Scotch tape. I first heard the Beatles and the Rolling Stones in the seventh grade when Doug Duda, the coolest kid in my class, showed up one day with a 45 of "I Wanna Hold Your Hand." It changed our lives. The photo of John, Paul, George, and Ringo with their mop-top haircuts and collarless suits symbolized the beginning of a new world of music, the first taste of what was to come in the sixties.

That fall, Miss Carpenter, my music teacher, started playing us records by Peter, Paul, and Mary, Bob Dylan, the Beatles, and the Rolling Stones. Music class was never the same again. Instead of singing songs out of old choir books, we listened to the new albums. She told us we could buy copies at Woolworth's in the new Coronado Shopping Center, near the school.

Rock-and-roll came alive in Woolworth's. When I first went there looking for records, I set foot in a part of the dimestore that I had never bothered to look at before. The record department was in the back of the store. The section grew in 1964 after the Beatles' first appearance on *The Ed Sullivan Show* and the release of *Meet the Beatles,* their debut American album. The first 45 I bought was Peter and

Gordon's hit, "I Go to Pieces." The first album was *Meet the Beatles.* I paid 49 cents for the 45 and $3.98 for the new LP.

I started spending all my allowance on records. Five dollars a week was enough to feed my music habit. I went into Woolworth's several times each week to watch the record section grow and to catch up on the latest releases. The white, wooden display racks were filled with records by groups from the first British Invasion—the Beatles, the Rolling Stones, Gerry and the Pacemakers, the Dave Clark 5, Herman's Hermits, the Kinks, and the Yardbirds. I wanted them all, but quickly fell in love with the Beatles. They were the only ones I bought in the first few months of rock-and-roll madness. I quickly piled up a stack of 45s.

The clerks at Woolworth's soon got used to the sight of kids hanging out at the back of the store. A clerk would stay at the back counter, making sure we were going to buy something and controlling requests to play the latest hits on an old mono phonograph the store had. The clerks played the songs only once, encouraging us to buy and then listen to them at home. We didn't protest very much because one listen was enough to convince us the new releases were great. We quickly grabbed them up, paid for them, and went to play them at somebody's house.

Of course, you had to find ways to convince your parents to let you use their old mono phonographs—ancient, bulky consoles that had not spun any hits since the heyday of Elvis Presley. Before we knew it, the latest envy was anyone in school who announced they had gotten a new record player as a birthday gift. My parents couldn't afford to get me one for several years, but their old console did just fine and outlasted many newer portables.

The beauty of buying 45s was not only that they were easy to get and quick to listen to, but they also came with

collectible record jackets. Each Beatle single came pack-
aged in an attractive sleeve with a different photo of the
Fab Four on it. When I had a pile of them, it was fun to
thumb through all the neat covers. With wear and tear,
though, many of my record sleeves tore and faded away.
Soon, I had a stack of 45s with no covers, but so did every-
body else. What we could never foresee is that, twenty-five
years after the 49-cent singles, those record jackets would
be worth hundreds, sometimes thousands of dollars to
collectors.

I loved to buy Beatle bubblegum cards, now also worth
a mint to fanatics. After picking up the latest 45, I would
stroll to the front counter where they kept the candy. Each
week, I would find a new set of black and white cards. I paid
12 cents for one slab of gum and five cards. Just like baseball
cards, the Beatles gave you photos of themselves with the
latest gossip and record information on the back. I collected over two hundred different cards. I don't know what
happened to them. They disappeared or got thrown away
when I graduated to psychedelic music later in the sixties.
If I still had those cards, I'd be rich.

Doug Duda was the first boy to imitate the card photos
and grow his hair a couple of inches too long. Two extra
inches in Texas of 1964 was *rebellious*. One day, he walked
into class with odd-looking, pointed shoes.

"What are those?" we laughed.

"Beatle boots," he replied with a cool look and a toss of
his bangs over his forehead.

"Beatle boots?"

"Yeah."

"Where did you get them?"

"Woolworth's."

The store's shoe department, small and specializing in

cheap tennis shoes that didn't last two weeks, had a surge of business when they got their first shipment of Beatle boots. It was the craze. We all found a way to get ten dollars for our first pair. Even if it meant going one whole week without buying a new album, we got a pair of Beatle boots.

Beatlemania kept the Woolworth's clerks on their toes as the look of the store got wilder by 1965. We had to walk through the fabric department, ladies' apparel, and the toy section to get to the enlarged record section. Beatle posters were everywhere. The display bins bulged with all kinds of popular music—Johnny Rivers, the Mamas and Papas, the Lovin' Spoonful, the Young Rascals, the Supremes, Freddie and the Dreamers. John, Paul, George, and Ringo grinned down at the competition because no one could keep up with their number-one hits and record sales.

If you were lucky enough to know someone in the store, you might talk them into giving you a Beatle poster for buying so many records. I got a few, but most of my Beatle photos and memorabilia came from the gum cards and *16 Magazine*. The teen-idol magazine had a revolution of its own as it went from articles on Fabian, Annette Funicello, and Frankie Avalon to interviews and scoops on Liverpool, the Beatles, and the nasty Rolling Stones. I bought dozens of issues so that I could cut out the Beatle photos and put them in my Beatle scrapbook, a project of imitation because Doug Duda had a similar book. The visual fascination with the Beatles may have had something to do with their rebellious look, a group of young men that boys my age wanted to imitate. We wanted to upset adults around us by growing our hair and defying them.

The height of Beatlemania lasted from 1964 through 1966. After that, Lennon and McCartney dropped acid and joined Sergeant Pepper's Lonely Hearts Club Band, a change a young music critic like me saw coming with the release of my two all-time favorite Beatle albums—*Rubber Soul* and *Revolver*. These albums showed how the Beatles spent more time with the complexity of their music in the recording studio, when they quit touring in 1965.

By the time we entered the eighth grade in 1966, many Beatle fans were caught up in the San Francisco sound, the second wave of great sixties music that would replace, during the fall of 1966 and through the summer of 1967, our rites of puberty symbolized by early Beatlemania. We went from the two-minute Top 40 hits to the elongated, psychedelic waves of the Jefferson Airplane, Cream, Quicksilver Messenger Service, the Thirteenth Floor Elevators, Country Joe and the Fish, and Steppenwolf. By 1967, the record department at Woolworth's stocked these new groups, but most kids were going to the new, independent record stores popping up around town. They were the "in" place to go because they sold black light posters, rolling papers, and incense. In some shops, you could find out who had "dope" for sale. Several record shops in El Paso did brisk business in cheap Mexican grass that went for ten dollars for a fat lid. Places like Lenny's Records and Budget Records and Tapes stole the crowds away from Woolworth's. It was a change none of us noticed because we were flying through the electric sounds of Big Brother and the Holding Company, Iron Butterfly, Moby Grape, Vanilla Fudge, The Who, and early Jimi Hendrix. This music was not around in the brief days of 49-cent 45s and Beatle boots—pure, early days that woke many of us as we held on to the last audio signs of our innocence.

The last album I bought at Woolworth's was *Rubber Soul*. I paid $5.98 for it. It was the new price in late 1966. I no longer bothered with 45s. Albums were it.

Rubber Soul was the turning point for me. I went from
teen worship of the Fab Four, which reached its height in
1966, to serious listening the following year. I grooved to
the Doors, the Electric Flag, Blue Cheer, Sly and the Family Stone, the Mothers of Invention, and the Grateful Dead.
I started paying attention to the meaning in John Lennon's
lyrics. After *Sergeant Pepper's Lonely Hearts Club Band*
was released in early 1967, any teenager who understood
John Lennon would not be caught dead in a store like Woolworth's, much less buying Beatle bubblegum cards or wear-
ing Beatle boots. The mature Lennon was not the same
moptop we had loved earlier.

I still have all the albums I bought in Woolworth's. Who
knows where the scrapbook is. I wore the Beatle boots for
less than a year, then threw them out. Woolworth's is now a
Walgreen's that stocks a few cassettes and CDs, but no albums. Vinyl records are extinct. The Beatle songs I hear on
CD sound totally different and eerie compared to the origi-
nals on the 45s and LPs. In remixing them with the new
sound technology, the record companies can't reproduce
the spirit of Beatlemania. It is lost forever. Traces of it can
be found if you pull out your worn-out vinyl records. The
pops, jumps, and scratches may call back part of the spirit.

I occasionally pull out my *Beatles '65* to stare at the
worn cover, thinking back to the rush of those Woolworth's
days, my cheeks bulging with Beatle bubblegum. Along
with millions of people all over the world, I was swept up by
Beatlemania. We never knew it would be so short-lived, had
no idea this early music was marking one of the most intense changes in American culture, a rapid change heavy
on the innocence of youth. In contrast, the music of the
later sixties was influenced darkly by the Vietnam War and
its punch on our psyche. The lingering power and influence

of rock music on my writing and life remain. It is immeasurable.

The dizziness of the early sixties is best symbolized for me by the Beatles' first movie, *A Hard Day's Night.* I saw it for the first time in late 1964. A gang of us went to the old Plaza Theater and were overcome by the electric atmosphere of hundreds of kids bouncing in their seats, screaming at the black-and-white images of the Beatles on the screen. Ringo's solo walk along the Thames River in the rain is one of the greatest sequences in modern cinema. His innocent stroll in 1964 looks like a calm journey before a greater storm that had not yet hit when the film was made. Going wild in the movie theater was euphoric. At the crucial age of thirteen or fourteen, it was important to discover how many kids liked what I liked.

After the matinee, several of us took the bus home and got off at the shopping center. We practically ran into Woolworth's and straight for the racks to see if the *Hard's Day's Night* soundtrack LP was in yet. We hopped down the aisles like the Beatles did in the movie and stopped suddenly when we spotted the police officer talking to a clerk and a kid we didn't know. The boy was in tears. The cop held a couple of Beatle 45s.

As my friends pounced on the five or six brand new copies of *A Hard Day's Night,* I was pushed aside in time to hear the clerk tell the cop how she caught the kid shoplifting the 45s. She told him she was surprised because the regular customers always paid for their records, bought dozens from her, and never caused any trouble. I didn't hear what the cop said. As I grabbed my copy of *A Hard Day's Night,* I saw the look on the boy's face.

I moved to the counter to pay. His look of envy and despair got to me for only an instant. I paid for the album. As I walked out of the store, the cop led the kid down the aisle. I don't know what the penalty was for stealing $1.80 worth of Beatle music. When I got home to my growing record collection and put the new LP on the old phonograph, I thought about the kid. I felt bad for a second, then forgot his dilemma on hearing the first guitar chords and John's clear voice. John's voice set me straight about the kid in the store. The power of the music and what it did to us all was more important than the plight of one kid with no money. This music was liberating us, but it was also planting the seeds for the narcissism that would follow in later years, a time of caring less about important things. I jumped up and down, did some air guitar, and counted the two hundred records I had for the millionth time. Every time I bought one, I wanted five more. Every time I left Woolworth's, I had to find a way to get money to buy more music. This was rock-and-roll and nothing could keep me away.

Guitar Picks

The smile on Jimi Hendrix's face makes the cover of the new book gleam in purple and throws feedback on the old vinyl walls of humming amplifiers. Thumbing through pages of musical scorn and wild notes, I have the tendency to go back and pull out the old LPs from the stacks of hundreds and hundreds of old albums. I wonder if the face on the cover of the new book is going to spin at 33⅓ or lift off the turntable, demand a new CD only, and quit screaming about foxy ladies and third stones from the sun? Where is the truth that Spike Lee is trying to get at, when he says he is the only one who can make a film on the life of Malcolm X? He can't get the real way there, can't be a down brother, until he makes a film about Hendrix. Follow Malcolm with Jimi, and the pretenders will leave the throne forever. Find someone else to package in those long, ugly CD boxes that can never match the heavy beauty, grace, and colorful cardboard majesty of good, old-fashioned vinyl records. In the middle of this song, this wailing for a language of musical notes, the Jim Morrison poems start pouring into my office. Poem after poem inspired by Oliver Stone's film. The poets sending them are good writers, but can't break on through to the other poem, because the half-dozen Jim Morrison poems that have entered the office are lousy poems written by good jammers, great poetic guitarists who can't get down and truly riff how Jim Morrison slapped us when we were in

high school. His death is one of the biggest rip-offs in the
music industry, because he is dead and there is no way anyone will keep him dead. Elvis, can you hear me? Both of
them sell more records now than when they were alive. So
what if I saw the Doors in concert in San Diego in 1970, less
than a year before Morrison gave his final scream in the
tub? The concert was awful and mesmerizing, the lizard,
stripped of his jacket skin, was not quite there as he was
stoned with matchbooks thrown from the crowd when he
asked for a light. He screamed that the women of San Diego
were lousy fucks. The crowd cheered that one, until he
stuck his microphone into the amplifiers and the explosions
deafened the crowd forever, shut them down as the band
burned through "When the Music's Over" and got out of
town fast. Now, they want to keep him alive and it will never
be over. Even the notes grow louder in their feedback majesty. Even the Thirteenth Floor Elevators are on CD, and it
is getting harder to find the old albums. I wonder what I will
do when they finally become extinct. I go to the large
wooden shelves and count the albums in my collection. The
record swap meet always has good ones. I read Link Wray is
finally being put on CD and it reminds me that I lack most
of Wray's music. I compose a list of all the sixties music I
want to rebuy on CD, while I play the rare 1969 BBC tape of
the Led Zeppelin shows, Jimmy Page's weird, heroin hum
on "Dazed and Confused" caused by him cutting into the
guitar with a bow from a violin, Plant's awful voice, magical
and spitting against the dread of Page's dark vision, the
ghost of John Bonham snapping on the broadcast, racing on
the tape with the speed of "How Many More Times." Thank
God the program avoids any version of "Stairway to Heav-
en," the one song by those gods I hate. I wonder how Page
got the barracuda up into the naked groupie as she lay on

the bed, the band testifying it was true in the book, all of
them laughing years before Page went into his reclusive,
Alaister Crowley–induced heroin sleep. It pushed him out
of the scene for most of the eighties, until his awful solo
album a few years ago, its black cover the mist that feeds
back on Page's huge amplifiers. I break down and buy my
first Neil Young album on CD, *Weld*, the three-disc live set
where Neil finally goes mad with amplifier wisdom to perform the loudest, heaviest music of his career, a frantic
dose of nineties music that most nineties music lovers will
overlook because Neil is too powerful for them, his black
Les Paul connected to the stage floor by underground mag-
nets. He admits in a magazine article that his crew drills
holes in every concert stage floor to feed special wires into
the belly of the auditoriums, so he can hook up the intricate
wires and electronic brains of his sound system—getting
the special sound that rips die-hard Young freaks as it has
for twenty-five years—an electric wind that knows no
direction, except the love of the ear and the pounding of
the rock-and-roll heart. The third disc in the set contains
a special 35-minute feedback jam called "Arc," one of the
biggest risks he has taken, one of those mad journeys Neil
loves to take, belching guitars and amps howling like the
Persian Gulf War has not ended and Hendrix's death is taking its own electric death-time inside Young's amplifiers.
The long feedback becomes the flattened lighting bolts of a
time that no rock musician will ever capture again, even if
"Arc" is the explosion it is supposed to be—cutting through
the swamps of sound that must be flattened to get to the
side that counts—the song bearing the hole of truth in its
reverberation—the guitarist who holds one guitar that has
never been played the same by other guitarists—one guitar
different in the spotlight—its neck and dials glistening in

the shattered walls and mirrors of a sold-out, standing-room-only concert crowd. I can't believe the CD sound, until I buy *Electric Ladyland,* and I am floored by the guitar on "Voodoo Child," the one Hendrix song I would take to my grave if I had a choice of one song to clutch forever, my bones shattered by the underground feedback buried with me. Yes, some CDs sound better, not all, but what do I do with those thousands of albums? I will never give them up. Extinction of the vinyl habit. I never thought the day would come when buying vinyl records would be an almost impossible act because record stores stopped carrying them. Even used record shops are cutting back on their three-dollar albums and stashing used CDs instead. How can I listen to Moby Grape, *On the Beach* by Neil Young, *Teaser* by Tommy Bolin, and the first James Gang album if they are not available on CD? If I store my albums, do I have to get rid of my worn-out turntable? I can't even find the right needle replacement for it at Radio Shack anymore. I feel better when I run across the CD of one of my all-time favorite records and rock bands—Quicksilver Messenger Service. Their first two LPs are released on compact disc. I can hardly wait to hear John Cippolina's growl on "The Fool"— the cosmic twelve-minute song that is the most important legacy of psychedelic music ever recorded. It is an orgasmic knockout—the CD version actually sounds better than the original because Cippolina's claws cut sharper and deeper in the fired-up sound. His wah-wah becomes the sound of God wailing from above—the growl on "The Fool" is God scraping his guitar pick across the chords of heaven, eliminating any guitar pretender from the stage, the incredible Cippolina drive emerging from the speakers as an electric ghost that has been buried for twenty-five years. I don't like the way the remix has changed the order of the songs on the two albums, but I admit placing "Acapulco Gold and Silver" right after "The Fool" is not a bad idea. The second song is another guitar tablet from God and has not been imitated or reproduced by any other guitarist since Quicksilver ended the first side of their debut album with it. I hate how they cut the long live "Who Do You Love?" to a lousy three minutes. That is sacrilegious! Even classic albums, lucky to be resurrected with the new technology, are not spared the nineties mentality about what should and should not be put on the CD. I program "The Fool" and "Mona" to play over and over, then fall asleep after the twenty-first spin of the songs. When I wake, it is late evening. The lights on my JVC mini-stereo blink and wave, waiting for me to program the stereo like the tiny computer it is. As I turn it off, I miss my old turntable, saddened by the idea of storing my albums forever, not being able to stare at the jacket covers anymore. Even Captain Beefheart's music is on the new discs. I can't believe they actually put *Trout Mask Replica* on disc. The weird Captain's voice cuts and deciphers the mountain cough of Zoot Horn Rollo's hyper guitar and Rockette Morton's dumping bass. I pop Santana's *Caravanseri* on the player and wait for the electric crickets to click into the timbales, bongos, and low wail of Carlos' guitar. *Caravanseri* is Santana's master work. I remember reading a classic Ralph J. Gleason review of the album in the March 1973 issue of *Rolling Stone,* one of the moments of great journalism and timeless music. This whole music rush, and the anguish of admitting CD technology into my life, brings me to my most cherished memory of the sanctity of rock-and-roll. It is about Bill, my long-lost best friend from El Paso, now a wandering alcoholic. He was the guy I grew up with, the two of us real close in the sixties and early seventies, when we lived and died by rock music each day. Bill loved the

Grateful Dead, Joe Walsh, The Who, and the Allman Brothers. Yes, the Allman Brothers—symbols of early seventies
love and death, drugs and brotherhood, distance and time,
sadness and grief, guitars with Duane Allman as the ghost
of memory, the haunting electric guitar pick of friendship
that I thought would never end. The early seventies were
years of dumb, drugged innocence, a time when we swore
rock music was clean salvation. Hanging out on Bill's farm
and getting stoned to "Whipping Post" was pure ecstacy in
a decade that brought numb existence and the cold departure from the burning sixties. Bill's father owned a horse
farm, a small, isolated place north of the Rio Grande, in
what everyone knew as the Upper Valley. Bill lived there for
several years, and it was our hideout, the place we could
escape from the responsibility of growing up, the "mel-
low" setting perfect for those years when cosmic cowboys,
pot, good music, and ambivalance fit the surroundings. We
loved that place, although Bill never had much privacy
there. On some weekends, people took riding lessons from
the woman who leased the stables from Bill's father.
Friends and strangers also hung out there, all of us finding a
way to get "loaded," the common response many people in
their early twenties gave to the first half of the seventies.
The farm was a sanctuary of both peace and music, property in the southern part of La Mesilla Valley, made for
young men who thought living in the Southwest was the
best thing you could do in life. Plus, we had our music! It
made all the difference and was a hell of a ride. Ask Duane
and Berry Oakley, the bass player for the Allman Brothers.
They both pasted their souls against the asphalt of time by
wiping out on those bikes, assuring their place in the halls
of rock infamy. I have not bought *The Allman Brothers Live
at the Fillmore East* on CD because the memories of my

friendship with Bill and those wonderful times on the farm
are too painful. We played that live double album over and
over, wore it out more than any other we owned. The wild
beauty of Duane Allman's and Dickey Betts' guitars, along
with the addicting fury of Greg Allman's timeless voice is
too much. I yearn for those days on the farm too often. I
may never come to terms with how the flash power of such
rock like the music of the Allman Brothers brought young
men, in their early twenties, so close together. The weeping
majesty of Duane's guitar added something to what we had.
His death at twenty-four was also our death. As we played
"In Memory of Elizabeth Reed" and "Whipping Post," we
tried to avoid the end of those days, putting off the inescap-
able fact that we were going to get older and go our separate
ways, despite having rock-and-roll music as part of our
lives. Yet when I hear "Whipping Post" on the radio, or occasionally play it on cassette, the beginning of the song tells
me our friendship is preserved. When the live version is
about to begin, Duane announces, "Here's a song from our
first album. Berry starts her off." Someone in the crowd
yells, "Whipping Post!" Duane answers, "Yeah, you got it!"
Berry's deep bass lines tear off and paradise on the farm
comes back, crashing and blazing out of Bill's enormous
speakers. I have not spoken to Bill in six years, don't even
know where he lives in El Paso. I relive those days through
my music and wonder if Bill has drunk himself to death. I
know the wailing cries of Duane and Dickey Betts' guitars
on "In Memory of Elizabeth Reed" are the yearnings for
that friendship, but I want those days in the early seventies,
not the lone wisdom of the nineties. The climax is when we
would blast to the sky with one of the greatest guitar solos in
rock history—the second section of "Whipping Post" on
the Fillmore album. Dickey Betts' shrieking guitar is the

closest I have come to understanding the heart power and importance of rock music in my life—how it has hurt me and given me joy. It has killed many of my heroes—Hendrix, Lennon, Allman, Joplin, Morrison, and Cippolina. It has helped to sustain the love for writing, teaching me how to write poetry by listening to rock music—sounds of razor guitars, the sounds of a world giving us beautiful noise to keep us from giving in and failing—the Allman Brothers, Neil Young, Jimi Hendrix joining Bill and me on the farm as the sun set a violent orange in the sky. Bill would pass the roach and pop open another can of beer—the cool evening raped by the high volume as Duane cut back in and took us to the peak of our friendship. These were weekends of getting wasted on the potent language of rock, getting older by hanging out, postponing the truth of the world by drowning every moment of time with the vibrating circle of electric weapons that Duane and Dickey twisted into the black night of La Mesilla Valley. Bill's huge speakers were mounted on the porch as the timeless towers of music and a brotherhood that would last forever, like the fourth or fifth encore where the spotlight hits Duane as he welcomes Jimi on stage. Neither one of them brings lighter fluid or motorcycle gas because their fingers are already soaked with the friction of their boiling arms, red hands and red guitars on fire, their red eyes and bleeding faces reflecting in the spotlight. The hurricane of the massive crowd turns up the volume on the crash of guitar mournings that feed back because those explosions, deaths, and timeless bonds from the frets and broken strings can never be recaptured on brand-new, remastered compact discs.

Go! T-Birds! Go!

The touchdowns come in a recurring dream. I am the fullback running around right end with the football, headed for a forty-six-yard touchdown run. The cheers in the Sun Bowl are deafening, thousands of football fans packing the stadium, our school colors of blue and gold clashing with the opponents' red and white. Waves of fans are on their feet, a sea of banners flying through the air because my brilliant moves give us the victory over Bel Air High School. We win the city championship 21 to 17. I am the hero. My fellow teammates stream onto the field and carry me off on their shoulders.

At other times, I am a middle-aged man returning to my high school to regain my old job of head manager of the football team, the Coronado High Thunderbirds. The head coach, who never ages, is there to welcome me back. During practice, I fetch footballs, repair broken face masks on helmets, tie shoulder pads, and help the trainers tape the players' ankles. Most of all, I need to laugh at the constant jokes thrown at me by the players.

They are the heroes and I am the peon waterboy, as they and the student body see it. I smile at the bigger players when they call me "fatso," waving me over like their slave. "Manager!" They yell as I run to them. I know what they want when they point to the ground. I bend and tie their shoes before one of the huge linebackers decides to knock me on my ass, or one of the elephant offensive linemen spits at me through his mask, a favorite thing for football players to do.

These two dreams of hero and wimp occur a couple of times a year. I have had them for twenty-three years, since graduating from Coronado High. I was the sports editor of the school newspaper and covered all the games, but I was more proud of my other job. For three years, I was one of the six managers of the football team and got a great, behind-the-scenes look at Texas high school football. It was more exciting because the T-Birds were city champions three years in a row. We beat every school in El Paso by scores like 70–0, 49–3, 62–7, but we also had close contests that we usually won. We lost only five games in three years, dominating the sport in El Paso in the late sixties.

I was swept up in "school spirit," a jock rah-rah mentality. I loved to write sports stories. In the process, I found my place in the pecking order of the social structure of the school. High school kids want to fit in somewhere. Since I wasn't an athlete or class president, and no girls would go out with me, my roles as sports editor and manager nourished me. They made the social rejections easier to take, getting me through the four years of high school, while implanting a deep, inferiority complex that is still reflected in my recurring dreams.

As one of the assistants, I helped the coaches run the team by doing odd jobs during the daily grind of after-school practices. The tasks ran from keeping the equipment in working order, to taking the dirty uniforms to the school laundry room, to handing towels to the players as they came out of the showers. The managers did errands, kept the locker room clean, photocopied playbooks, and of course, pulled the water pump around the field so the players could drink during the hot fall practices. We were the water boys.

The high point of being a manager came during the Friday night games. We were masters of the sidelines. While the heroes pounded their opponents for a six-yard loss or caught four touchdown passes, we paced the sidelines with the coaches. During a time-out, two of us would run to the huddle with towels and squirt bottles full of water or Gatorade. A sweating player would stand or totter, helmet pulled up on his head. He'd open his mouth wide, not say a word, and we would squirt him. The huge linemen loved to grunt and drip sweat as they towered over us, sometimes wiping it off their faces with pudgy, taped hands and flicking it at us. They loved to spit the Gatorade back in our faces. The cool wide receivers, running backs, and quarterback waited calmly for the referees to whistle for play to resume. We ran off the field.

Throughout the game, we kept a constant check on the equipment, ready to give a player a new helmet or shoulder pads. If someone limped off the field with an injury, we jumped at the chance to help the trainer.

During a game, the most prestigious reward a coach could give a manager was the chance to work the headphones that kept the sidelines in communication with coaches up in the press box. If the coach got furious over a botched play, he would yank the headphones off and throw them at one of us, then scream at his players and pace the sidelines. The lucky manager fantasized about being a coach. We would say a few words to the confused coach upstairs, who was busy watching the action through binoculars while trying to talk to the bench. Most of the time, this coach would tell the manager to shut up and get off the air.

We played ten regular season games, five in our home stadium, five on the road. The bus rides back after a victory on an opponent's field were fun. The managers had to make sure all the footballs were in the bags, the equipment stashed on board, and every dizzy player accounted for. We rode in the back of the bus like the second-class citizens we were. The heroes rode in front with the coaches.

Most of the football players on the T-Bird championship teams were talented, pampered, and arrogant. A few were good, straight-A students who loved to play the game. They didn't have the win-or-else mentality of most players. Those types were rare on the team. The nicest guy was Charlie, the quarterback, whose outstanding academic achievements made up for his average skills at football. He was friendly to me and we loved to talk about rock music. So was Manny, a wide receiver, and the only Chicano player on the team. He grinned from ear to ear as he caught many touchdown passes. The two of them were the only ones who never made fun of me.

The rest of the team was something else. The most hateful and mean players included Phil, a linebacker; David, a defensive end; Jack, the star running back; and Rick, the dumbest guy on the team but the best player in the school and a blue-chip player in the state of Texas. He played fullback, center, and tackle. He loved to grab managers by the neck and shake us like rag dolls, squeezing until we turned red and pleaded for mercy.

The worst abuse came from guys like Phil. Besides punching us for no reason or demanding we tie their shoes, guys like him were experts at verbal abuse mixed with a good dose of racism. "Hey, what's a dumb Mexican like you doing being a manager?" he would ask me from the sidelines during practice, waiting for his turn to get into the lineup. "Hey, fatso! We've got too many managers. I'm telling Coach to get rid of all the Mexican managers." I was the only Chicano manager.

The only time he might have appreciated managers was once in a time of trouble. During a close game with our cross-town rival, Irving High, Phil got knocked down on a crackback block by a tight end. As an Irving running back raced around him with the ball, another opponent came and put a foot through his face. After the whistle blew and the pile-up cleared, Phil lay motionless on the field. We called time-out and ran to the seemingly lifeless figure. His face was a bloody mess through the broken mask. I helped him to his feet. Two of us held him up and walked him off the field. He gave me a painful, glassy-eyed look when he took off his shattered helmet. It was the only time he accepted my help without putting me down.

The worst humiliation came during my junior year. It was a hot afternoon drill in the first week of practice. One of the coaches made me hold one of the blocking dummies during a play. Dozens of players stood around watching the first-team offense and defense practice, but he made me stand in as the left defensive end, clutching the inflated dummy like a pillow. As the quarterback took the ball from the center, I gripped the dummy and braced myself.

Dickie, a senior running back and Phil's rival as chief torturer of managers, came around the right guard and slammed into me, instead of walking the play through as instructed. Despite the cushion of the dummy, he knocked the wind out of me. I flew backwards about ten feet and landed with a thud on my back. I lay gasping for air until the coach ran over, grabbed me by the belt, shook me, and sat me up. I rose slowly to the loud laughter and applause of the players. I heard several "dumb Mexican" mumblings in the huddle as I limped off the field.

I accepted the pain and abuse because I thought it was part of the game. I was doing my job for the team and the school. I liked the coach. My loyalty to him and my pride on being part of the team gave me strength to get past the cruelty of the players. Nothing could top the thrill of having a winning football team and being part of the daily operation, an insider who wrote good sports stories from the vantage point of loyal manager.

The one time I was recognized by the team and the student body came after the greatest game the T-Birds played in my four years of high school. In October of my senior year, we beat Artesia High School 14–13, ending their twenty-seven game winning streak. They came to our stadium as two-time defending New Mexico state champs. It was the fifth game of the season and we were also undefeated.

The Bulldogs were a big team. They wore bright red uniforms with black helmets and black face masks. Our blue and gold jerseys paled next to their striking ones. I sensed we would win the game because I had never seen the players prepare so hard. Even Rick worked intensely, taking home the extra playbooks the coaches gave the team. Many players got in trouble with other teachers that week for overlooking homework and studying plays instead, an extra effort I never saw for other games.

As the overflow crowd thundered, "Go! T-Birds! Go!" the team surprised our opponents by playing tough defense and running the ball for the first two quarters. It was 7–7 at the half. The powerhouse Bulldog offense, averaging 35 points per contest, had never been held to one touchdown so early in a game.

The air was thick with anticipation for the second half. It was the manager's job to run to the dressing room to call the team back onto the field. I raced across the end zone, circled the track and ran to the dressing rooms behind the grandstands. I flung the door open to find the coach leading the kneeling team in prayer. I hated to interrupt, but the referees got on your case and could penalize you if the team came out late. "Time to go!" I yelled. The sweaty, dirty players shouted in unison, "All right! Let's go!"

The second half got off to a shocking start when the Bulldog quarterback connected with his right wide receiver for a 72-yard touchdown pass on the first play from scrimmage. I flung my towel to the ground as the quick, short receiver raced past the last T-Bird cornerback. The home crowd grew silent, but quickly recovered their spirit when Phil and Jim broke through the line and blocked the extra point. The score stood at 13–7 through the rest of the third quarter and most of the fourth.

With four minutes left in the game, Charlie hit Manny for a 17-yard gain to the opponent's 26-yard line, the deepest T-Bird penetration of the second half. From there, with thousands of spectators on their feet and the sidelines vibrating with tension, the T-Birds clicked off two running plays to the 18-yard line. First Jack, then Rick carried the ball to the 11. With 1:37 showing on the clock, Charlie surprised everyone with an unexpected call and gave the ball to Rick, who ran up the middle of a startled Bulldog defense for the winning touchdown. The extra point was smooth and true.

Starting on their own 18-yard line, the Bulldogs had 1:04 left, but their incomplete passes on every down were not enough. The final gun popped, and thousands of T-Bird followers raced onto the field. Hundreds of them knelt and joined the team in the traditional post-game prayer. A roar erupted when the victorious team rose, and helmets, banners, and happy players flew through the air. They grabbed the coach and carried him off the field on their shoulders.

This was the football highlight of high school life, not only because we had beaten a good team, but because the response to my story in the paper the following week was overwhelming. My headline read "Bulldogs Remember T-Birds!" It was one of the best stories I ever wrote. The emotion, thrill, and the insider point of view gave it an edge that few sports stories contained. It won a high school journalism award later that year.

I knew it was good, but I saw it as just the latest article when I wrote it. When I walked into the locker room the day the paper came out, the coach was in his office and called me in. Three other coaches sat around grinning. Coach said, "You are really a fine writer. This is one of the best things I've seen on the team. Congratulations." He shook my hand. The other coaches rose to do the same. I was speechless and embarrassed. They had never acknowledged my stories before.

"I got several calls from some of the teachers today," the coach continued. "A couple of them read your story to their classes and told me several of their students were in tears. They were crying and proud about the team effort and the way you covered our great victory. Thanks, Ray."

I walked out of the office, embarrassed at all the attention. Charlie, Manny, and even Rick told me they liked the story. Some of the other players just looked at me without saying a word. None of them abused me that week. They were busy practicing for the first division game on the road to our next city championship.

◆ ◆ ◆

The recurring dream where I score the winning touchdown always happens in the championship game against Bel Air, never against Artesia. I don't have to take the field against the Bulldogs. I've had my victory over them. It doesn't have to be part of the dream where my touchdown run against Bel Air replays itself, over and over again, like the game films the team studied every Monday.

The other dream comes back more often than the triumphant touchdown run. There I am, returning to the school twenty years later to help the coach to victory. There are new, younger players on the team. For the first time in the recurring cycle, Charlie, Phil, Jim, and Rick are gone, replaced by new faces of people who do not abuse me. They look up to me. I am the veteran manager who keeps coming back to help the coach mold another winning team for the school. They respect me and run through their drills without putting me down or making me tie their shoes. I don't know what to do with this new version of my dream. I wonder why the faces of the players have changed. I have waited for this version where the players accept me as their equal, not as a star running back or one of them, but as the quiet manager doing his part to make sure the team is ready on Friday nights.

I wait for another kind of dream, too, one where I return to the school as a spectator in the stands, free to watch a new team score touchdowns, yelling and clapping because I enjoy the game from the bleachers for the first time. No racism. No abuse. I don't pace the sidelines anymore.

California, 1976

I soar toward the sea, away from the desert. It is a walk along an empty beach, the cool October ocean stretching dark blue over the horizon, meeting a line of gray, a shadow of sky rising and falling with the shock of leaving home to live elsewhere for the first time, new territory away from the suffocating desert. My bare feet stick in random patterns of sand, cross other footprints; the beach is pockmarked with trails in all directions. A roar of water raises my head, forces me to meet the legions of waves that break into tiny, crystal globes shooting into the air, disappearing to rain down as mist kissing my arm and chest.

The waves erase the footprints to let the globes fall onto clean, undisturbed grains, brown and green showers of particles that I last saw on the back scales of a strange lizard, seaweed and driftwood advancing toward shore with their own tails. I look up at the few clouds as they vanish into thicker mist. I want to recall a description of desert suns, but the dream tells me this is a different sun falling off the edge of the world. It is not the hot ball that I left behind to blind other natives of the dry desert. I hear a shout and look up to a place on the high, dry dunes. A woman sits in a wheelchair, her body motionless, her legs wrapped in a large, green towel.

Mary is in her wheelchair, under the umbrella I put there for her, insisting she is comfortable. She won't let me set her down on the blanket in the sand, even though she has allowed that before. I tell her the sand would feel good under her, but she shakes her blonde head. I get down on my knees in front of the chair and touch the cold metal wheels.

Mary closes her green eyes, then opens them to stare at me. She moves her lips silently, as if sending me a kiss. It is a whisper I am not supposed to hear or acknowledge. A brief rush of panic crosses my heart, a slamming beat like the day I crossed the New Mexico border, knowing I was never coming back.

How do I know what to do, how to be, when I have never been with anyone before? I embrace her, hold her tightly while my head hurts. I wonder why we met this way, her marriage falling apart because of her husband's cruelty over her illness. My chaos in the blindness of a twenty-four-year-old breaking the magnetic wave of desert and cactus that have lanced the heart for too many years.

I run down the beach in late evening. The sun is a pink ball painted on the water, double circles between old desert loneliness and the new coast, a first lesson by Mary like the *cuento* of the woman born with two heads, living her life with one head silent and hidden behind her, covering it with a coat to look like a hunchback. One day the hidden head wakes up and screams for freedom because it is time to light the fires across the desert, to let people know that old women with two heads have more to say than people with only one.

The sun spreads against that old family legend like a cloud of red pressing against my idea that it is impossible to write about a new landscape, even if Mary says the new poem is good. I know these sea poems do not enter the world the way my clay, cactus, and snake poems leave it. Too many greens and purples, too much confusion over which is dry rock and cottonwood, which is juniper and moss on the cliffs.

The rigid shock of being caught in fresh territory is still too much, my shaking over departure, crossing the highways over Deming, Benson, Yuma, and La Mesa. My desert used to be a sea long before it laughed with the idea of a young, naive exile. I write about mountains, the first image showing me it is time to run down the coast, past the spreading moss, to the suffering woman.

The first time is interrupted by a fleeting moment, a voice saying, "It is time to go home. What is here on the shore is not yours." The story of a handicapped woman with two kids, hanging on after two brain tumor operations, cannot be told at this point. It is like the other *cuento* of the young boy wandering the streets of Juarez with six toes on each foot, the extra ones brown and dirty in his barefoot searches for a handout around the *mercado.* His talent at selling himself is the key to his survival, a way of showing the *turistas* the extra toes make him a good street dancer, bringing a toss of quarters out of pity and wonder.

In my dream of West Coast mountains, I am too young and scared, tripping in the deep sand of my own dance. Her small, fat hands touch me for the first time. There is a shadow emerging from this older woman beneath me, moving under me. I am running on the beach, wondering why she wants to be alone. I run out of breath, drop to the sand, and see a scorpion oozing in the mud. I know it is only my loss of desert. I lie outstretched to catch the mist, happy for a moment of safety, the promise of being able to create and write in a new place—so much water and the fear of falling. I stand closer to the edge of the continent, shaking at the edge of the cliffs. I want to fall into the lost desert volcano, clouds of ash obscuring the giant arms of cactus that impaled me, held me prisoner in the volcano for two and a half decades.

I walk the beach in the humid night with the taste of love on my lips, a tiny voice yelling that the first time is not supposed to be like this wall of shock over a paralyzed body. Anything can happen during the pounding of the waves. Don't hesitate to the adventure of it. She can do anything a normal woman can.

Her estranged husband disappears for weeks. He always comes back to check on her, she says. It is the pattern. Do not worry. I watch an old couple standing on the jetty in the wind, the two of them swaying on it. The rotting planks creak, huge waves roll to splash them, forcing them back from the edge, making them turn toward me.

The two strangers are in love in their old age. They move down the beach with wet clothes, legs in stride, arm in arm. The seagulls screech and bother me for the first time, reminding me of pages of torn newspaper floating in the dusty wind of San Jacinto Plaza in downtown El Paso, of faces of poor *Mexicano* children looking up at the sudden flapping of wings, of dark pigeons rising in the dirty plaza. Seagulls bother me with their constant shrieking over the sand; they remind me that the dirty plaza contained a fountain and a pool where the city kept alligators as a tourist attraction. They kept them floating and baking in the downtown heat for years, until the alligators died of old age or were removed because too many people threw trash at them. Two of the oldest alligators were injured when someone shot arrows into them one night, the alligators of San Jacinto Plaza, those monsters of childhood memory rising out of the concrete fountain to grab me and place me on this newer beach.

Mary said it was fine and I felt better, warmer with the

repeated visits to her house. Then, the purple light I often see across the waters returns, a slant of color rising through the waves. It is another attempt at writing about the other strange lizard I found in my backyard, the one with the bright red head and dull gray body, the only lizard blossoming that way, making me see further into the magic of the desert, into the hot sands that petrified, eroded, and left their own vast oceans for others to excavate.

It is an attempt at writing poems away from the barrier of desert mountains that don't belong between my lines as they tower over my stanzas. I tear up the new poems, my hands shaking, Mary's hands shaking, the poems melting on the rocks, glowing in the night as if the paper caught the fire of the red-headed lizard that flew across the coast in search of the one who followed it around the backyard as a boy.

The first time she held me, I cried. There was a mirage, a double illusion. One woman rolling up the beach on wheels, letting go as I arrived on a coast whose gray mass of sea looked like the moon, distant travel on distant planets, hot craters of desert volcanoes falling back to keep me inside. The tide rises to cover thoughts of the desert which continued to expand despite my departure, the tides soothing the reflections as dreams of troubled sleep when you first move to a place you can't write about.

There were no friends for months. I wanted to keep it that way, then I saw the ad in the San Diego newspaper from someone needing help with a handicapped person. With great freedom, the woman in the wheelchair turns to me as the giant spray smashes against the rocks, hurls the circling birds away from the canyons and cactus. I kneel in front of the wheelchair, run my hands through the cool sand as she stares at me, letting me know that the sea brings things to her and always washes them away.

Confessions and Communions

My life in the desert was shaped by my strict Catholic upbringing, by the fear of sinning, of my soul turning black to seal my fate of going to hell. Baptism, catechism school, my first confession, and holy communion—images of fear and respect for the man on the cross. I am surrounded by votive candles, *santos,* flowers, Padres reciting *la misa* in Latin—a chanting, humming sound I did not understand when I sat in the hard pew between my mother and grandmother, the heat of July suffocating the hundreds of people inside the churches of Santo Angel where we worshipped, or El Calvario where I was baptized, or El Sagrado Corazon where I was confirmed.

The suffocating atmosphere of *la misa* blends with images of old women kneeling, reciting rosaries quietly, crossing themselves, walking slowly to the altar to light a candle. I follow my mother down the aisle of the long sanctuary, the deep stillness of the church broken by the echo of our footsteps on the concrete floor. The place suffocates me with ancient smells of the dead and the ever-faithful. I hear occasional weeping from some of the women who kneel at the altar to pray for lost relatives, for a son killed in a gang fight, for the poverty of the barrio that forces men to go farther away in search of work.

On the way out of the church, I always passed the confessional, a frightening, dark closet where I would have to confess my terrible sins to the mysterious Padre who sat in the middle chamber, his face hidden by the wire mesh stretched across the tiny window separating the confessor from his holiness. I dreaded going into the confessional. My months of preparation in catechism class were filled with a growing fear over the approaching day.

Catechism class at Sagrado Corazon Church is a blur. All I remember is the nun scolding us for not memorizing the Lord's Prayer correctly, yelling at us because we did not know what page we were on in the booklet.

The boys wore white shirts and black trousers for the first confession. The girls could be as colorful as they were on Easter Sunday. We lined up at the back of the church on a hot spring day, the rows of pews at Sagrado Corazon filled with our families. On signal, we marched down the aisle, our knees shaking as we tried to remember the right words we had to say to the Padre. We were blessed as a group, then led toward the pews near the confessional where we knelt to pray and wait our turn in the closet.

I started to hyperventilate as I waited to confess the evils of my young life. I watched each boy and girl enter the booth on each side of the Padre. I wanted to catch their expressions as they came out. I got dizzy watching them emerge because all had pale, shocked looks on their faces as they survived. They knelt to say their penance. I wondered what awful punishment the Padre had ordered.

My turn came. I rose slowly, dizzy, then managed to get by two other kneeling boys. I entered the cool darkness of the booth, shut the curtain, and knelt. I was startled when the Padre slid open the window, the signal I should begin.

"Forgive me, Padre, for I have sinned," I began as I heard him cough on the other side of the screen. "This is my first confession. I hit my sisters. I disobeyed my mother by not picking up my room. I thought about the Devil. I fought with my cousin and pushed him down the stairs." I went on and on, until I ran out of breath and terrible sins. I waited for the voice to condemn me. I can't recall what the Padre said. I sank into a black hole, straight through the confessional to hell. I could not tell him I felt that way because it was a sin to think of Satan in church. This meant I had sinned before I had even left my first confession.

"Say five Our Fathers and ten Hail Marys, my son." I did catch that. I crossed myself as he muttered a prayer I did not understand. Then he blessed me. I stumbled out of the confessional, my shirt soaked with sweat. I blacked out for a few seconds, felt my mother take my arm and lead me to an empty pew. I sat down without a word. We both knelt to pray. I pulled my rosary out of my pants pocket and started my penance.

The rest was easy. After the whole class confessed, we marched up the aisle and knelt at the altar. The Padre performed several rituals in Latin before he turned, blessed the gathering and proceeded to give us our first wafers of holy bread, the final gift from God saying we were forgiven. The wafer stuck to the roof of my mouth. I flicked at it with my tongue until I swallowed every bit of it.

After the service, I went home with a white soul and tried not to think anything bad, hoping my brief thought of sinking to hell in the confessional would by overlooked by God. I pictured my pure soul inside my head as a white cloud with black dots covering it each time I sinned.

From that day on, I feared and despised going to church. Those years of attending *la misa* with my family were filled with excruciating boredom from long, hot ceremonies I didn't understand. Our constant genuflection before the pews, the kneeling to make the sign of the cross, and the whole Sunday was dominated by my fear of sinning and going to hell.

Kaleidoscope of great Catholic fear: The time I almost fainted when I was overcome by the incense the Padre waved during a special mass. My father had to take me out of the church in the middle of the service. It was the only time the two of us ever went to church alone. The Sunday I fell asleep, only to be slapped awake by an old woman who kneeled to my right, my mother intently praying her rosary to my left, not even losing a beat as a stranger abused her child. The return for my second confession a horror because I was forced to go back into the closet by my mother, only a few weeks after my first confession. The longer period between confessions seeded a deeper guilt. The smell of the holy water rose as I dipped my fingers into the bowl and rubbed my forehead with it. Add the great guilt of walking around with a huge ash stain on my forehead on Ash Wednesday. Finally, one day, around the age of fourteen, it hit me that my family had stopped going to church. I had not entered one in months, a period that lasted twenty years.

The final part of the kaleidoscope is like the stained-glass windows in the sanctuary high above me. After several years of loneliness, I met Ida and got married for the second time. A few months before our wedding, in a Lutheran church, I had a dream that was both nightmare and salvation.

I am asleep in bed. Suddenly I hear a loud buzzing above me. I look up to see a large red claw, a gnarled foot, sticking out of the wall. A creature tries to grab me with its enormous claws. I sense evil. To the right of it, I see Jesus crucified on the cross, the crucifix hanging on my bedroom wall. I must choose between good and evil. The loud buzzing hovers above me. I stare in horror at the giant claw next to the bleeding Jesus on the cross. A bright light appears between the two apparitions. I must choose between them.

I try to wake up, reaching the point where one gasps awake after a nightmare. As I moan to open my eyes, I choose. The light moves toward Jesus. Before the beam reaches the cross, I wake up, making noises, fighting for breath. I lay in bed exhausted, shocked, worn out from my visions. I have made my choice, but part of me isn't clear what it means, concerned I woke too soon.

The dream flings me back to my childhood, and to my mother. She leads me by the hand as we run up the stairs, late for *la misa*. We bless ourselves quickly with the holy water. The church is overflowing with worshippers, hundreds of women draped in colorful shawls and scarves, many of them dressed completely in black. There are also hundreds of men in suits and clothes of the *caballeros*. Colorful statues of La Virgin de Guadalupe and darker ones of San Martin de Porres vibrate in the death-like haze that hangs against the high ceiling, the corners of the enormous church clouded in the smoke of prayer, incense, and the secret suffering of the worshippers. The sizzling claw and the subdued Jesus on the wall above my bed show me my mother and me taking the last two seats in the back of the hot church. We kneel to make the sign of the cross, and I see the shrouded face of my grandmother floating above me. The second and third faces of old women I do not recognize also appear, their skeletal cheekbones glimmering with the fleshlike tone of the Virgin Mary's statue that cracks higher above their praying faces, the three shrouded women holding heavy, black rosaries in their trembling hands, the vision overcome by the sickening smell of incense, a signal for me to sit back up as the crowd of Catholic worshippers fight for air in the sanctuary. Their bodies push

against each other when they kneel to pray. The tight rows
of people sit back against the hard, wooden benches with
one low hush of dark clothing, one low rustling of rosary
beads that make the claw disappear forever. The smell of
sweat, breath, and the clicking of rosary beads among the
flickering candles covers us in the wavering light of the
faithful. I reach for my own rosary, a tight knot of twisted
beads I have carried in my pants pocket since the first day
of entering the expanding air of hazy whispers, those final
sounds that always lead us to the end of our chanting.

Abuelita

I call her *"abuelita"* and pray to her voice, saints of love and forgiveness, the movement toward ceremonies and red rosaries made from rose petals. San Antonio y San Martin are after me to thank the spirit that still moves over the Franklin Mountains and desert in search of the hot soil, the boiling earth giving birth to chants and *novenas,* to *Ave Maria y mi Padre Diós.* She is the *abuela*—gray and old in the land of our house, the old woman of torn adobe, of ringing church bells on Sunday and the bedroom full of statues of saints, pictures of La Virgin de Guadalupe, the crosses on the walls turning black, infinite oaths to the invisible life of the heart, the one beating across the Rio Grande, south, toward the twilight side.

She tells me how it was before *la revolución Mexicana,* how her mother took her in the horse-drawn wagon to the *mercado* in San Luis Potosi and bought her cream-filled *gorditas,* which she loved to eat as a little girl, before the guns and the thunder brought her north, before she was separated forever from her family.

My grandfather Bonifacio Canales died in the desert of Arizona in 1941, three weeks after Pearl Harbor, when they first noticed the American bombers flying west over the Superstitious Mountains toward the war. She tells me how he worked the railroads for thirty years, alongside the other Yaqui Indians in the 112-degree heat. They repaired the tracks and sometimes killed a dozen rattlesnakes per day as the crew moved down the blistering tracks, hammering away, killing the snakes to make progress across the desert. She says Bonifacio drank too much, never went to see a doctor, and died suddenly one morning. He never saw his dream come true, his goal of building the huge house he wanted for his family, and the chicken farm he talked about starting so that he could get his three sons to gather the eggs and sell them in Benson. She can still remember the funeral train making the journey from Fort Thomas, Arizona, to El Paso.

She has shed too many tears over her sons and daughters, too many tears for grandchildren she raised as kids while their mothers worked hard, took care of them before they grew up and left her in the barrio. She tells me about the miracle over the divorce when my father and mother went their separate ways after thirty-two years of marriage. She points to the picture of La Virgin de Guadalupe, shows me the wrinkled corner in the framed photo. One morning, she saw that the picture of La Virgin had moved inside the glassed-in frame. It had turned upside-down by itself and she had felt the pain. She prayed to La Virgin without straightening the picture. The next day, she found out about my parents. The whole family prayed in her house after my father left for good. The following day, when she woke up, the picture of La Virgin was straight with wrinkled corners. The photo had righted itself, and the struggle to accept the divorce began.

The red rosary beads are made from rose petals pressed into hard, round shapes. How many petals does it take to form one tight bead? *El rosario* gives off the sweet smell of roses when held to the nose. The flowery scent fits the prayer and the chant, the whispered oath and the silent "Amen." El rosario comes from Spain, brought to the barrio of El Paso by Padre Martinez, who gives the few he has to close patrons of *la iglesia de Santo Angel*.

I keep el rosario in a white plastic box, circular in shape, with a picture of a beautiful Spanish garden painted on the lid. Open the smooth box and the smell of roses covers the moment of prayer, the kneeling before the crucifix on the bedroom wall, the fingertips rolling the beads in the sweating palms of shaking hands. *Un Padre Diós y diéz Ave Marías.* One Our Father for miracles to be done on earth as in the heaven being sought each night, each step from one red bead to another. The chain of ten Hail Marys for the guiding oath for sinners wandering the desert. I am taught to believe this way as a child, the only way to survive in El Paso.

El rosario is twisted in the night of prayer, red beads in the red candlelight, waiting for the red dawn, when the prayers are answered. In the morning, el rosario is found under the pillow, burned under restless sleep. There is no one in the bed. The hands, cold in the morning, reach under the pillow for el rosario, to wear it down further. The friction between the fingertips and the beads touch between body and spirit, a lifelong dependency on prayer, until the final Amen is whispered one morning.

El rosario is made to last for years, passed on to the family, to a granddaughter or son. Years after the death of la abuelita, it is found tucked in a drawer, the white box hidden inside the cardboard case holding the family *Biblia.* The one who finds it picks up the box and opens it.

The smell of roses, so well preserved, is freed into the room. A hand lifts el rosario, amazed at the dark-red beads clicking against each other. They are held to the nose. Hands do not hold it like she used to hold it. The crucifix is no longer on the wall. There are no candles in the room.

The new hands put el rosario back in the box. As it is placed in the drawer, the smell of the roses vanishes from the room, now absent of hands, prayers, and beads that shone in the candlelight, years ago, when wrinkled hands pointed their fingers toward the crucifix, asking to be lifted into heaven.

With Neruda in the Desert

Pablo Neruda died on September 23, 1973, three days after my twenty-first birthday. I always pay attention to significant events that happen on the twentieth of September each year. In 1973, I missed Neruda's death because when I was twenty-one, I did not know who he was and was unaware of his accomplishments as one of the world's greatest poets. I certainly didn't know Richard Nixon, Henry Kissinger, and the CIA were behind the murder of Salvador Allende, Neruda's friend and the popularly elected president of Chile. Allende's death preceded Neruda's by a few days. His assassination at the hands of Augusto Pinochet's right-wing army was the catalyst for Neruda's death, even though cancer had gripped the poet for several years.

In 1985 I discovered more details of Neruda's death after reading Ariel Dorfman's essay on Neruda's last days. Dorfman, a Chilean writer in exile, wrote that during the coup, a military operation was carried out on Neruda's three houses in Santiago and Isla Negra. Pinochet's men found Neruda sick in bed at his famous home in Isla Negra, a small town west of Santiago. The soldiers ransacked Neruda's library and priceless collection of sea shells and model ships.

Dorfman writes how the major in charge confronted Neruda and became flustered at facing the famous poet. The major excused himself by saying, "I'm sorry, sir, but we have been informed that there is something dangerous here." Legend has it that Neruda answered, "Very dangerous indeed. It's called poetry." A few days later, Neruda died on his way back from Santiago after his ambulance was stopped by soldiers and delayed for three hours.

When I read Dorfman's essay in 1985, I was already a poet deeply affected by Neruda's poems, his life, and his love for the world. I had read dozens of his books translated into English. I had also read his work in Spanish and felt I knew his work well. Not long after Dorfman's essay was published in *Granta* magazine, a startling new book of Neruda's poetry appeared.

The Stones of Chile (White Pine Press, 1986) translated by Dennis Maloney, is an unusual collection of poems about the stones and rocks, amid cliffs of the rugged, coastal terrain of Isla Negra. The poems are Neruda's most dense and metaphysical. They weave their power through jagged rocks and ledges, rising through the sea as a celebration of the naked earth. The idea of the stones and rocks penetrating every aspect of life shook me because it was exactly how I felt about the desert of west Texas and southern New Mexico.

Rocks and *arroyos* of the Chihuahua desert lifted their heavy weight and dropped it into my poems. The solitude and sheer power of the vast desert is the same force Neruda's stones hurtled at Isla Negra.

In the winter of 1986, I returned to El Paso for a six-week stay to complete two book manuscripts, but I wound up discovering that I had also come back to confront the desert landscape and to try to understand why it was so prevalent in my early work. My newer poems were different and I could sense their release from the desert.

When I travel, I carry a handful of poetry books with

me. The most important one in recent years has been James Wright's last book, *This Journey* (Vintage, 1982). As I packed for the trip to El Paso, I decided to take only a few books since I wanted to concentrate on finishing the manuscripts. I chose *This Journey* as my lone companion, then went back to the shelf and added Robert Bly's *Selected Poems* (Harper and Row, 1986) and *The Stones of Chile*. I think I grabbed the Neruda because it was the most recent translation of his work I had received. Reading it on the plane to El Paso, I felt the same powerful impact that I had when I opened it months earlier. As the plane dipped over the Franklin Mountains and into the El Paso airport, the site of the brown, barren peaks took me to Neruda's stone work. I hoped the sense of *rock* in Neruda could help me come to terms with my own sense of desert.

Between periods of intense writing at my mother's house, I drove through La Mesilla Valley north of El Paso, to hike in the area around the Organ Mountains. Their peaks rise thousands of feet above the desert floor. They stand east of Las Cruces, New Mexico, and guard the southern end of *La Jornada del Muerto*, a barren, one-hundred-mile stretch of desert historically significant as the burial ground for many Spanish *conquistadores* attempting to cross it, with little or no water, in the sixteenth century.

One cold December morning, I walked through a rough area of low hills several miles west of Victorio Peak, the mountain on U.S. Army land alleged to be the site of the Lost Padre Mine. The mountain, named after one of the last Apache chiefs who held out against the U.S. cavalry, was off-limits to civilians. I did not want to go near it; instead, I was drawn to the walls and canyons of the other hills. Several of them bubbled up like bloated volcanoes, dark-red monuments to isolation reminding me of Neruda's poem

"The Lion." He writes, "A great lion arrived from afar: it was huge as silence, it was thirsty, seeking blood, and behind his investiture, he had fire like a house, it burned like a mountain of Osorno."

In the cold mist of the desert morning, the ragged cliffs of these red hills looked like lion heads and manes rolling out of volcanic bodies. I looked up at the cliffs as I walked over the dirt trail away from my car. The natural cuts and shapes of desert hills amazed me. The miles of yucca, ocotillo, and Spanish dagger cactus gave the hills a distinct, threatening look.

As a veteran of desert hikes, I knew these hills were not easy to climb. Hikers used to the grassy fields and forests of the Rockies are surprised at the obstacles faced in climbing a desert hill. Thousands of cactus and loose rocks force hikers to use careful movement over the terrain. A desert walker literally must zig-zag around sharp cactus every few feet. Rocks and dirt tumble down at each step. Temptation to take short cuts through a Spanish dagger field can be dangerous. I have been stranded among Spanish daggers before. I have walked into a dagger field only to find that I can't get out without getting stabbed. Walking out of the daggers is like running an obstacle course of booby-trapped knives.

But that December day, the hills were not too difficult because mesquite bushes grew abundantly and spread the cactus farther apart. I had no idea why I chose these hills. The desert gets very cold in winter and its wonderful aura of colors is muted. But the red sandstone cliffs in front of me kept their color year-round. They protected several canyons opening a few hundred yards from where I stood.

I stopped at the top of the first hill and turned to look back down at the highway. A distant gray fog covered La

Mesilla Valley. I longed to see the ocean waves of Isla Negra come pounding through the valley. In my own poems, I had compared the desert to a sea several times. I looked around and found proof of the desert's geologic life quickly.

I kicked a mound of earth packed by rain and picked up a dusty slab of rock. Brushing the dirt off the surface, I found dozens of tiny fossils in the stone. I held the common prehistoric remain of the great ocean that covered this area millions of years ago. These fossils were easy to find after a good desert rain. Arroyos of the Chihuahua desert were full of these miniature colonies.

The shell creature brought me back to Neruda. I thought of the animal in "The Portrait in the Rock":

> Then, once, on a stormy night,
> with snow weaving
> a pure coat on the mountains,
> a horse, there, in the distance,
> I looked and there was my friend,
> his face was formed in stone,
> his profile defied the wild weather,
> in his nose the wind was muffling
> the howls of the persecuted.
> There the man driven from his land returned,
> Here, in his country he lives,
> transformed into stone.

I returned to the desert to pick up a fossil as I had done many times as a child. It was easy to find signs of old life. Fossil hunting was not a challenge, yet it was difficult for me to face the desolation and the isolation of the desert amidst this ancient life.

The cliffs above me scared me in a familiar way and made me wonder how far I was from Perillo Springs (Little Dog Springs). This last passage from Neruda brought back the story of the waterhole in La Jornada named after the dog that found it. In 1598 a party of Spanish conquistadores found themselves crossing this stretch of desert without water as they explored the Rio Grande on the way to discovering Santa Fe Pueblo. The river meanders to the west. Explorers risked crossing La Jornada due north to save a hundred miles, shortening the journey by several days before joining the river again. After several conquistadores died on that journey, the party camped in La Jornada. One of their dogs wandered away from camp and returned the next day with muddy paws. The soldiers followed the dog and found the water. Perillo Springs no longer exists. It was swept under when Elephant Butte Dam was built to control the river north of here.

As I stared at the cliffs around me and held the fossil in my hand, I wondered if the dog was petrified somewhere around here. I wondered if the fears of the early explorers were the same kind I felt, off and on, in my years of wandering the desert alone. I carried water with me in a canteen, so it didn't matter if I wandered far from the river. Four hundred years after that dog got thirsty, the Rio Grande is more of a controlled channel than a true river. But thirst for water was not the kind of yearning I felt in the desert.

Every time I hiked the desert, I felt fear. But fear of what? Was it little dog fear? Fear of the unknown? As I stood alone on that cold morning and gazed up at the twisted rocks, a deep silence pushed against my chest. The yucca plants stuck their arms out at me, each one a different length, sheltering rocks and boulders under them. Was there something behind those rocks? Did a huge rattlesnake wait for me there? Did the crashing waves of the sea at Isla Negra move giant rocks aside to release a terrible truth into Neruda's earthy poems?

How did he handle the immense power of the rocks? How far into their subterranean roots and cracks did he have to sink to find peace beyond their space and matter? How far did I have to wander in the desert to find why these rocks and cactus always pulled me back, called to me with their silence, yet allowed me to handle my fear and wonder through my poems? Fear and wonder. Perhaps that was it. Fear and wonder.

Years ago I went hiking with a New York poet friend who had moved to El Paso to attend the creative writing program at the university. We found ourselves near Cottonwood Springs on the far northwest side of the Franklin Mountains. It was his first time in the desert. As we walked through the cactus, we talked about poetry. He grew quieter as we hiked. Finally, we stopped above a deep arroyo. I told him it was a good place for a rattlesnake nest. "I'm not worried about snakes, but why is it so quiet out here?" he asked nervously. I sensed that he was overwhelmed with the immensity of the desert. It was a reaction that I found in many people who admitted that they loved the Southwest, hiked in the desert regularly, and found themselves getting uneasy "out in the middle of nowhere." When they returned home, some admitted their emotions gave them a kind of rush among the rocks and cactus, followed by a sense of peace.

Suddenly I heard a noise behind me. I turned in the direction of the canyon. I couldn't hear any birds, no sign of the common vulture, but I heard something. I approached the canyon. The cactus thickened before a dense growth of mesquite. I spotted what made the noise. Several rocks and boulders were piled over a small cottonwood tree growing at the canyon entrance. They must have tumbled down the cliff recently, but their thunder was not what I heard. The clicking noise came from a broken branch tapping against another branch. The dangling branch was freshly broken— I could see the green slice where the rock had cut into the bark. The boulders shaved most of the limbs from the stunted tree but did not tear the trunk open.

The tree stood like a huge candle in the middle of a stone cake. It is a strange comparison, but the fallen rocks had landed in rough layers around it. They seemed to form a circular barrier of solid red rock that I would have to climb to get to the tree.

I sat on one of the rocks and noticed that the dangling branch was still. Without wind in the shelter of these cliffs, how did the branch make noise? I flexed my fingers in my gloved hands and waited for the sun to rise over the chilly cliffs, but the December mist would take hours to lift.

As I sat there, my earlier fear diminished briefly. I felt a great distance from my poems, from El Paso, even from Neruda. His poems were still with me, but his life in Isla Negra was so different from mine in the desert. Several tall yucca plants grew across from where I sat. Some were broken and split from rocks rolling through them. Here I was with my red rocks different from Neruda's black rocks, yet all the rocks were erected from the same source, a fire deep underground, molding Neruda's stone poems and branding my desert poems. The fire made me abandon the desert, only to return years later and sit inside the red destruction of these old volcanoes. I had never been in this part of La Jornada before, but I knew it was the guided spot to come and visit with Neruda and our rocks.

I had left *The Stones of Chile* at my mother's house, but I knew this passage well:

> Hips of stone in the desert.
> Here the walker fell on death.
> Here ended the journey and the traveler.
> Everything was sun, thirst and sand.
> He couldn't stand it and became silent.

My desert poems are full of silence. They describe "the journey and the traveler" and they talk about different kinds of death, historically and metaphorically. Most of all, they surge out of me in the great thirst, a yearning to leave the desert in a quiet way. The "hips of stone" fell off these cliffs and flattened the cottonwood, the yucca, and the desert itself. The stones rolled and expanded the desert for hundreds of miles. Cactus grew after the stones moved and challenged travelers for hundreds of years. Where were the nearest bones of conquistadores, lost in La Jornada? The stones rolled and crushed them into pumice. These red hills emerged the same way Neruda's rocks reshaped the Chilean coast.

The desert reformed my poems, took them over, and used them for its purpose of expansion and spiritual penetration. Then, it cast me out, not in a biblical sense, but in the same way Neruda described his stone poems: "The coast was strewn with these extraordinary presences of stone and they spoke to me in a hoarse and drenching language, a jumble of marine cries and primal warnings."

Desert rocks spoke to me. They made the cottonwood branches speak to me. As I sat on a rock and looked up at the cliffs, which hung closer to me, I understood their language. They told me that I had lived in the desert for twenty-five years because it took that long to decipher the language of stone that says you must fear the immense landscape, get inside it, be pierced by its knives, and come out stronger. The drenched tongues of rock prepare you for the world by offering their kind of solitude. As I sat with those red rocks, I realized that solitude was a state transforming itself from stone language to poetic speech.

I had to fear and live in the desert because, like Neruda, the great thrust of rocks in my life was a gift of discipline, spiritual and artistic, needed to survive and be in the outer-world. The primal warning was that I could not stay and hide in the desert forever. Like this cottonwood hit by falling rock, I had to break and go on to a new life and different poems elsewhere.

I rose from my cold seat and decided not to enter the canyon. I heard the branch tap again. My fear rose and fell. I felt less cautious as I climbed down the trail to the high-way. The mist hung lower against the walls. I spotted several yuccas and Spanish daggers growing out of the cliffs, up high where nothing could reach them.

As I moved down the trail, cliff rock and stone let their guard down to allow cactus to sprout. The cactus that popped through the steep walls pointed down at me from high above. They were the waves that Neruda describes in *The Stones of Chile*—movements of vibrating water and earth responding to angry rock and stone shifting under the ocean. I felt the same weight as I walked down the hill toward a desert highway that would be moved, someday, by the tide of oncoming rock.

Weeping Saints

The months in 1991 and 1992 bring reminders that something is happening with my Catholic faith—the strict religious upbringing I had in El Paso no longer recognizable. The mass is no longer given in Latin, and modern Catholic churches have fewer statues of saints. The Church quit demanding, years ago, that any woman entering the sanctuary wear a scarf on her head. But the new Catholic church is in contrast to things that happened these last few months. Several incidents of weeping saints and apparitions have been reported throughout the Southwest, so-called miracles in which hundreds of believers insist that statues of the Virgin Mary and Our Lady of Guadalupe shed tears, tiny rivulets of water forming on their smooth, carved faces.

There have been recent accounts of Our Lady appearing on a shower curtain in an old house in Laredo, and on an apartment wall in Las Cruces. That one drew my mother and two of my sisters to stand in line with several hundred other believers to catch a glimpse of the acclaimed image in New Mexico.

The latest event is the weeping statue of the five-foot tall Virgin Mary at Our Lady of Guadalupe Church in San Antonio, two blocks from where I work. This happened in June 1992, and was well-documented in both San Antonio newspapers, accompanied by photographs of hundreds of people packed into the church. It took place right before I

visited El Paso for a second time in two months. During the
first trip in April, I had realized that the spiritual world of
faith, family bonds, and individual conflict is never static. It
adds richness to its mysteries as it creates real occurrences
in times of transition, when one family generation passes its
traditions to the next.

With the weeping statue standing in a church near my
office, these miracles get closer to frightening me because
they are connected to my visits to El Paso. The time I spent
with my grandmother and aunt offered further proof that,
as the ones I love get older and prepare to die, the faith that
held my family together and influenced my escape from El
Paso may be dying with them.

Our traditional Catholic mysticism is ending, or at least
emitting unusual signs of spiritual upheaval, best illus-
trated by the hundreds who flocked to the San Antonio
church to witness the weeping statue. Most of the curious
are Mexican Americans raised the same way I was—loyal
Catholics who run to the church because crying saints are a
reminder that they must hang on to the past and have faith
as the century ends. They will not give in to the modern
church. Its new ways of operating deny the power of the
faith that built these churches in thousands of barrios in the
Southwest.

In San Antonio, Father Tony Ozzimo, assistant pastor at
the West Side church, first noticed the watery liquid on the
face of the statue and thought it came from a leak in the roof
of the old building. A woman who tried to clean the statue
wiped the first signs of moisture away, but the statue kept
weeping. People who came to see it agreed it was a miracle.
Maria Dora, age 65, told the papers that the Virgin Mary
was sending a message. "It is a message warning us of the
perdition of the world. She is trying to tell us to repent for

all of our sins." Dora is not far removed from my grandmother's generation. I am not surprised to read that she is celebrating the tears not as a miracle, but as a somber warning.

I return to El Paso in the spring of 1992, after being away for several years. I find the religious faith of the desert and the myths of sacred religion have been changing with the eroding barrios. Torn-down walls of old tenement houses give way to the one where Julia, my eighty-eight-year-old grandmother, lives with my aunt Consuelo, her seventy-six-year-old sister. The red-brick, one-storey building is made up of eight small apartments, my grandmother's screen door the second one on the right.

Julia sits on her bed, a near invalid who must walk with a cane, although she hardly moves anymore. After the embraces, kisses, and tears for a long-lost grandson, we sit quietly as she tries to recall everything she can about our family. Favorite memories and stories are told to me, over and over, funny and sad tales I have heard before. They are anecdotes repeated about my mother, my aunts and uncles, my nephews, and my sisters. I sit in a hard wooden chair trying to hold back the tears, knowing my grandmother has only a few years left to live. Her face has grown thinner, the once prominent nose sagging with final age, her long, white hair tied in a knot behind her head—an image I have known my entire life—a length of hair rare among modern women, yet common to older Mexican women who preserve the habits of their native Mexico. She doesn't look ill, but I know that this is one of the last visits because she offers a gift to me.

She pulls out two rosaries and hands them to me. She says the one with the black beads is from my first communion, a rosary she has kept for thirty years. The second is one of her favorites that she got in church many years ago.

I take them because it is a final passing on.

The bright green walls of her bedroom shine in the early afternoon sun, two of the walls saturated with dozens and dozens of calendar photos, prints, and paintings of different Catholic saints—San Antonio, San Cristobal, San Lorenzo, Our Lady of Guadalupe, La Virgin de los Dolores. She has collected them for decades, the walls of every house she has lived in lined with the faith of old Catholic beliefs, ancient family ways dissolving with each younger generation.

My aunt Consuelo sits next to my grandmother. They tell me how upset they are about the Catholic church changing so much over the years. They point to the statues of the saints to remind me that old icons and symbols are the only things left from the days when the mass was recited in Latin and the priests truly cared for the people— helping the poor, decorating the altars with candles and a rich variety of saints. My aunt Consuelo tells me that the new priests at Santo Angel church across the street have removed all the saints from the altars. They've quit giving food to the poor and keep the church locked until Sunday services.

As I hold the rosaries in my hands, the sweat fills my palms. I am sad, not at their disillusionment over the church, but at the fact that El Paso has changed beyond what I could imagine. The solid faith we knew growing up dissolves as we approach the new century. I didn't know I was coming back to El Paso to be given the family rosaries.

We are interrupted by a loud knock at the door. I have to tell them that there is someone knocking because they are both hard of hearing. My aunt gets up slowly and goes to open the door for Martita, a friend of theirs from Juarez, someone they have not seen in over a year. Her surprise appearance adds to the intense religious air that hovers over the room. I look at the beautiful statue of San Antonio, then turn to greet one of the most strikingly ragged and worn faces I have ever seen.

Martita is a fifty-four-year-old beggar woman. She has been wandering the streets of El Paso for twenty years, searching for hand-outs of food and money for her family, who live in a *colonia* of Juarez, one of hundreds of thousands of Mexicans trying to find ways to survive along the border.

"¡Ay! ¡Julia! ¡Consuelo!" Martita says in a high voice. "¿Come están?"

She greets them after carefully setting two plastic bags on the floor. My aunt and grandmother are surprised and glad to see her because this beggar woman lives from hand to mouth, day by day, never knowing when she will eat again. It depends on how much food she can carry on her daily, illegal crossings of the Rio Grande. Most of the food she finds is dug out of dumpsters and trash cans in the alleys of El Paso.

The three women hug and exchange small talk. I watch Martita's face closely because its dominant Indian features are unforgettable. She is a low, squat woman with a round wide face like the pre-Columbian rock statues I saw in an exhibit of Mexican art in a San Antonio museum. Her face is a pale red, almost light brown, one of those faces you might encounter in a dream of old women coming to bid you farewell after long lives—the moment they turn superstitions, myths, and their statues of saints into your possession.

Could the face of Martita be the same face I saw once, years ago, when I wandered the streets of south El Paso, drunk and nearly blinded by the fourteen beers Bill and I drank in Juarez, both of us stumbling young men afraid to leave El Paso for a better life elsewhere? We had crossed the Stanton Street bridge and were looking for Bill's truck in the heat of a Saturday afternoon. When we found it in a crowded parking lot, I saw an old woman lying in the dirt against a brick wall. As I swayed and managed to climb into the truck, she sat up and propped herself against the building, only three or four feet from my side. Her dirty face was wrapped in a torn yellow scarf, the swollen nose and red eyes distinct from the wrinkled, brown skin of her unforgettable features.

She stared at me, and in that moment I knew she came from the deepest root of mesquite, the thickest slab of adobe, and the dirtiest tide of the border river—currents beyond my control that made me rage, as a young man, at how we could get so easily lost in the alleys of the barrio. I stared back at her, my dizziness able to contain itself for the one instant I knew the face of that woman was the face of one lost ancestor I would find in each desert trek and every wild course I would take through the crumbling neighborhoods of El Paso.

Bill started the truck and backed out of the space as the old woman held a trembling hand up to me. He veered crazily across the dirt lot, throwing clouds of dust against this apparition. I leaned out the window to see her arm up, her hand open, her fingers clutching the air, the woman disappearing into the ground as we escaped. Even in my drunk state, I knew she was begging and tossing something to me at the same time.

◆ ◆ ◆

Martita sits with a grimace and wipes the sweat from her brow with her arm. My aunt and grandmother watch in silence as she makes herself comfortable. Martita wears a thick wool shirt with long sleeves and dirty polyester pants. Their blue cloth is faded and torn at the knees. I can't see the color or length of her hair because it is tied and hidden under a red scarf wrapped tightly around her head.

I sit and listen to the three old women exchange small talk about the heat and how hard it is to keep going each day, words I hear repeated, over and over, each time I visit. I debate whether I should leave and return the following day, but stay put when I hear Martita end the chatter by telling us where she has been recently. I don't move because I notice a change of expression come over the faces of my aunt and grandmother.

Martita tells us she has been in the Juarez hospital for ten days. She ate a piece of fried pork someone gave her in a plate of left-over food and got violently ill. Her son carried her to the hospital because no ambulance is going to come to the squalor of the colonias. She doesn't know what hit her. The doctor told her something in the spoiled meat almost killed her.

Martita shakes her head and keeps repeating, *"Gracias a Diós. Gracias a Diós."* She thanks God for saving her and tells us that the large, glowing rosary she hangs over her bed at night saved her. One of the former padres at Santo Angel gave it to her years ago, blessed it with holy water, and told her that the beads glowed in the dark. Martita prays to the radiating Christ on the rosary each night. She believes that its green glow is the kind of light she will see when she passes into heaven one day, Christ shining over her because she has the strength to survive and find food each day. She admits she was lucky to recover from the food poisoning and the dangers of being a patient in one of the worst hospitals in northern Mexico.

My aunt and grandmother shake their heads sadly,

mumble something I can't hear, then offer Martita a glass of iced tea. My aunt rises, goes to the kitchen, and fixes tea for all of us. My grandmother asks Martita if she crosses the border every day. Martita adjusts the scarf on her head and nods. The U.S. Border Patrol has caught her three times, held her for several hours, but then let her go. Her children worry and wait until past midnight for their mother to walk the night streets of Juarez. She makes her way home alone through miles of Third World neighborhoods. My grandmother is concerned about Martita crossing the swift Rio Grande rushing under the international bridges between El Paso and Juarez. She wants to know how Martita manages to cross the river twice a day.

My aunt returns with the tea in time to hear Martita tell another story, the kind I don't want to believe, but know is true because the spiritual bonds of the borderland are breaking. Religious beliefs of my family and the people of this area interlock between tragedy and the triumph of the soul—the boundaries of strict Catholic faith influencing what we see and do not see across the desert.

When something is revealed, it is a sign that my years of absence from this area have not changed everything. There are things still rising from the Rio Grande and its waters, the source of the holy drops sprinkled on me when I was a boy making my first confession and communion—perhaps the same source for the tears of the weeping saints.

Martita reaffirms this by telling us she fell into the river three months ago and was saved by the *coyote,* the man who extorts fees from illegals to let them cross in his flimsy raft each day. She was also saved by an old man who miraculously kept her from drowning. We stare at this crumbling woman when she says she did not drown because an old man with a cane appeared above the water. He told her to reach out for the arms of the coyote in the boat.

The river was moving very fast that day. The low raft was crowded with seven people crossing toward El Paso. It was six in the morning and they were all headed north to find work, another day of survival, meaning they had to pay one dollar to the man who controlled the raft.

They were half-way across the river when the raft tipped sideways and Martita fell in. She was swept under the raft, then came up gasping for air. She was quickly pulled several yards from the raft. As she turned to see if she was close to the shore, she saw the old man floating on the water. *"¡Era San Cristobal!"* she cried.

The old man held a cane and pointed to the raft. He wore a white beard down to his stomach and was dressed in a black coat. Martita knew it was Saint Christopher, patron saint of travelers, telling her which way to go. Before she knew it, the coyote steered the raft to where she was and quickly pulled her in. She says she would have drowned without San Cristobal's appearing to help her get back on the raft.

My aunt and grandmother make the sign of the cross. The room is silent. I listen to Martita's low wheezing breath and wonder how this beggar woman has survived through the years. She senses the heavy silence, then asks my aunt if she has any aluminum foil with which to wrap a paper-plate full of spaghetti with meat balls that she found behind a restaurant.

She pulls the food from her plastic bag and hands it to my aunt, who hesitates, makes a face, but realizes it is the only food Martita has found that day. I assume they will feed her while she is there, but I am surprised they don't offer her a meal. Would the beggar woman be offended if my aunt and grandmother offered her their food? My aunt returns with Martita's scraps wrapped in foil.

She gets up and thanks my aunt for the foil. "*Ya me voy*," she tells us and picks up the plastic bags from the floor. It is time to move on because she has told us enough. Recounting her near drowning makes her restless. For someone they have not seen in months, my aunt and grandmother don't seem to mind that she has stayed less than half an hour.

I watch silently as the three old women exchange hugs and final whispers, secret mumblings I have never been able to interpret among older Mexican women. Perhaps they are blessings and words of wisdom acknowledging that it is okay to depend so much on their faith to get by each day.

Martita turns to me, smiles with her wrinkled eyes, and says "*Vaya con Diós.*"

I nod and don't know what to say to her. She turns slowly as my aunt sees her out. I hear the rustle of the plastic bags as Martita steps through the door. They exchange a few words, then the rooms fill with silence. My grandmother sits quietly and waits for my aunt to return.

I use Martita's departure as an excuse for my own exit. I need to go back to my mother's house and pack my suitcase for the return flight to San Antonio. It has been a short visit. In recent years, my trips to El Paso have been short, but this one has revealed things I did not expect to carry back. The two rosaries are a surprise because my grandmother has given me other rosaries in the past. These two are the most important. The string of black beads has contributed to this chance encounter with Martita, someone I will never see again. I could go to the river and look for her among the thousands who cross every day. I may find her in the coyote's raft, or might hear from my grandmother that they fished her out of the river, her years of misery finally over.

I rise and kiss my aunt and grandmother good-bye, go through the awkward farewells I find so difficult when I see them. My grandmother cries. I wonder if it is the last time I will see her. After Martita's visit, my departure is made easier because I think of the glowing Christ on her wall at night. The dozens of saints on my grandmother's walls also glow at night. Even from hundreds of miles away, I sometimes open my eyes in the middle of the night and see the outline of San Martin and the sheep, dogs, and horses surrounding him as he raises his kind hands, their thin bones moving like the lanterns of those signaling the newly dead which direction to go, which wall to pass through as they cross the river the same way Martita does, bobbing and gasping for air because the floating saints, in their light, save those who open their eyes in the mad rush of Rio Grande water.

I know the church across the street will crumble and lose its young, modern priests before my family and the poor of the border lose their faith. I know this as I leave my grandmother to her tears and her walls of saints, dozens of them watching over her.

After I return to San Antonio, my mother and sisters scold me during a long-distance phone call for not visiting the weeping Virgin when I had the chance. By the time I return, the miracle is over. The Virgin has stopped crying. The barrio is filled once again with senseless gang killings. If the church makes the five o'clock news now, it is because its priests are organizing summer programs for the neighborhood kids, their attempts at fighting the gang problem. Religious news is off the air. The mobile TV vans and the reporters with their long microphones stop coming to the neighborhood.

In a few weeks, the weeping statue is forgotten by the

people of San Antonio and south Texas. For a few days after
she stops crying, I think of Martita each morning as I go to
work. I park my car in the lot that only recently had been
filled to capacity with cars of the curious who walked across
the street to see the weeping miracle. Now, in the everyday
routine, the lot is empty and makes me picture Martita digging through the dumpsters there. Would she find anything
of value in trash dumped so close to the holy ground of
faith? If she had seen the weeping Virgin, would her life of
poverty have changed?

Martita would be welcome here and probably find a
more hospitable church than the one in my grandmother's
neighborhood. The priests of Our Lady of Guadalupe
Church are not as contemporary in their thinking as the
priests in El Paso, who lock my aunt, grandmother, and
Martita out of their church. Any weeping in El Paso would
come from the homes whose walls are covered with saints,
weeping that would be so private and so powerful that the
release of its forces could reach me hundreds of miles away.

There will be no public crying of saints in El Paso
churches this year. Too many changes prevent it from happening. The weeping was a sign of faith at the turn of the
century, when a crying statue could draw people together.
There was faith when an old man hovering over the Rio
Grande saved a poor woman from drowning. Most of all,
the weeping of the statue, like the weeping my grandmother does each time I visit, was the way to draw the faithful together. The power of tears is one of the most potent
forces rising from an increasingly faithless Southwest.

Memory Fever

There are motions with mouths of water sliding toward the Rio Grande, continents to explore alone, deserts to confuse the mind and spirit. There are fires at night that signal to those high above the planet to come down and cross the Don Juan de Oñate Trail, to retrace the lost steps of the *conquistadores* who saw the walls of gold before they fell at the hands of the people. There are voices, doubts, and desert heat, an ocean of sand to cross in search of the unmarked trail, footsteps petrified since 1492, the path of the one who holds knowledge of the border and what happens to families who live here. There are those who want to establish the new tribe on the same mountains that rise to the stars, keep the black curtains of family secrets buried in the rocks of the Franklins, the Organs, and the Sangre de Cristos. There is the train coming to El Paso in January 1942, the widow and her children riding in the car with their belongings, the grandfather's casket on board, the family leaving the harsh wilderness of the Sonora desert of Arizona for the isolated struggle in the Chihuahua desert of west Texas.

✦ ✦ ✦

I wanted to travel through my desert of hope and vision, discover the distant territory I had never visited. The animals in my dreams wander there. The rattlesnake coils and shakes its song from under the rocks. I listen to it without

stepping back, wanting to record a scientific account of a
muscular movement, a venom that can't be analyzed in a bi-
ology text, a nature study of this barren land. I listen to the
rattle. It will not strike me in the heart. At long last, I admit
it will not hit me in the center of the cactus flower, the red
pear *los ancianos* cut with machetes to feed *el niño* the
sweet meat, watch him grow beyond the outstretched lines
of thorns.

The coyote knows I am alive. It is one of the earliest
sounds of the desert I carry, the coyote on the hill across
the street from my house, whining at three in the morning
as I lay awake, wondering why the railroad tracks are miles
from the house, the distant train whistle drowned by the
sudden whelp and call, a howl my *abuela* said could never
harm me because the coyote is no longer the drunk, the
borracio, of the desert. The coyote reforms his ways to sit
on top of the desert hill across from my bedroom window,
waiting for me to acknowledge I know something about
him, a boy who has not yet read that Indians considered the
coyote "God's dog" because of its magic life and its sacred
throat escaping when it is detected. The soul lifts from the
bed and wants to dance to the howling, but is too afraid to
acknowledge the howling. As I rise, I do not know that coyotes put out fires, that many of them have been observed to
extinguish man-made fires in the desert by stomping on
them with their quick paws.

◆ ◆ ◆

The bats swirling across Carlsbad Caverns neither approach me nor land to invade the mystery that others have
created. The bat flashes its tiny black wings and brushes my
head as it vanishes toward the silence of the desert night. I
run into the darkness without knowing how to silence the

space in the corners of the adobe room. My abuelita looks over my shoulder, a red rosary in her hands. She is laughing at my quiet moment, every word a prayer, my fear of whispering in the center of the room coming from a small boy afraid to sin because she tells me my soul will turn black *y El Diabló* will come for me *y La Brujá* will come for me. I will go to *El Infierno*, a boy cast out of the desert that he has wanted to abandon his whole life.

◆ ◆ ◆

The oily smell of healing leaves fills the room as my grandmother opens the bottle and pours the green liquid into her hands. I lie in bed with throbbing legs, the powerful odor of the broken twigs and gnarled leaves fills the room. She sits on the edge of the bed and rubs me down, her warm hands pouring a warmth that cures me, black leaves soaking in the bottle for years, secrets of the mud and vine fermenting to vaporize into the bones of pain. She massages my aching legs with the thick liquid, tells me the story of the lizard man who first showed her a bottle of healing leaves, the strange man she encountered in San Luis Potosi, the *curandero* who knew trees were the silent healers who would save anyone. She calls him the lizard man because he hunted and sold huge green lizards and the rare black Gila monster, reptiles stiff and dripping on the stick he carried into the village.

The lizard man taught her about transferring the fumes of the leaves onto the body of those who are loved. Innocent arms and legs are burned with the seeds that replant and rejuvenate inside the bottle, until their fire is released into me one night, an evaporation from trunk and stalk to the moving muscles of my body which rises from the bed moments later, the urge to run from the overpowering fumes forcing me out of the house. I stand on the porch, watch the stars of the desert night disappear over the spreading lights of a growing city, wondering why the smell of the leaves is the smell that makes me want to kneel down and dig in the moist dirt.

◆ ◆ ◆

The ability to ignite in sudden interruption is the lighting of the magnificent candles flashing into fires of faith on the altar, the Day of the Dead bringing visits to Concordia Cemetery in search of a misplaced family grave, where my *abuelo* lies buried for fifty years to disintegrate family ashes into the desert where we root our own paths, trying to break through the soil.

Concordia Cemetery is the oldest in El Paso. For years, it was notorious for hiding the unmarked grave of John Wesley Hardin, the famous gunfighter and outlaw who was killed in a downtown saloon in the 1880s. They found and marked his grave in 1984, but forgot to mark my family plots—the crumbling cement markers and wire crosses harder to find among hundreds of old graves. Josefina Gonzalez, my father's mother, lies there, having died when he was five, casting him out to shine shoes on street corners of the barrio so he could feed himself because his father wouldn't. Benito Canales, my mother's stillborn brother— buried somewhere in Concordia because my grandfather sent Julia to El Paso to give birth. They lived in Arizona in the early 1920s, but he wanted his son to be born in El Paso. Julia Silva, my great grandmother I hardly remember, the one who took them in when Bonifacio died, welcoming them to El Paso in the midst of the second World War.

Concordia Cemetery stands under the freeway, the site of one of the few dreams I recall from childhood, where I walked the rows of graves with an old woman dressed in black, perhaps my mother or grandmother. I could never see her face because it was covered with a long black scarf and shawl, her dusty black shoes looking like my grand-mother's, but resembling those of a stranger—a thin wom-an with bony arms and legs appearing through the sheer black dress she wore. She led me past the strange shapes without a word, although I heard whispers wavering out of the ground. She moved past the flowers, the crosses, and the cracked headstones—a woman with no face searching for a grave, the boy walking behind her realizing, for the first time in his young life, that this fenced-in area con-tained secrets no one wanted to pass on to him—dreams of burial mounds, burial plots, families standing around the hole as someone drops dirt into it with a shovel, a dream of walking past endless rows of graves, acres of fallen ground sinking deeper into the earth—one of the first places in the desert the boy would have to uncover, someday, in the infi-nite dreams of waking in a harsh desert that has saved its vast miles of sand for him and his mourning dreams.

◆ ◆ ◆

What if I found a skeleton buried in the desert? Would I run? What kind of skeleton, human or animal? Dig it up? Feed it to the sandy wind? Stare at it, then calmly walk away? I would kneel, cover the protruding bones with dirt, say a brief prayer, build a fire, and spend the night there, lis-tening to the coyote and the owls, count the hours and wait to hear the clicking of bones and the scraping of approach-ing footsteps in the dirt.

◆ ◆ ◆

The silence of humiliation is the strength of silence, how I learned to be strong when the coach called me a lazy liar, claiming I quit doing exercises when he turned his back. It was fifth-grade P.E. class. We lined up in rows on the blacktop and did jumping jacks, push-ups, and other exercises before breaking into our softball or kickball teams. Coach was mean and called me "fatso," saying the fat ones never did their exercises. One time, he stopped the whole class, made them stand in the hot sun while I did extra push-ups. He stood over me to make sure I did them. Then he sent me home with a note to my mother, saying I always quit when he turned his back. She wrote him a note in return. I gave it to him and trembled as he read it and started cussing me out. Knowing my mother, it must have been something about her guilt over her disobeying son, how he would lose weight to keep up with the rest of the boys. He made me run extra laps around the football field because he didn't like my mother's note.

I never cheated, never stopped jumping or doing push-ups when he was distracted or looked the other way. I never stopped, but huffed and puffed, my silence the strongest barrier against the jeers and cries of the other boys who got mad when Coach made them repeat the jumping jacks because I was not doing them right. Coach taught me the strength of silence, the desire to strengthen my body in the heat of the day, the waves rising on the melting asphalt as I got down on my hands and knees, rising up and down to get stronger, up and down to know how to live within the silence of a fit body.

◆ ◆ ◆

The fever of time came when I worked as a lot boy at the used-car lot where my father was a salesman. I had the job for several summers, earning one dollar an hour, then one fifty a few years later. Smitty's was one of the biggest used-car lots on Dyer Street, the place where my father toiled for years, hardly making enough money to put food on our table. I learned to drive a stick-shift by having to jump inside each car and start it every morning. I drove them from the neat rows into the car wash, learned to jump-start the ones with bad batteries, discovered the dirty tricks of the trade when the salesmen pulled the odometer cables from the cars so they could drive them. Once, pulling a car out of the wash in reverse, I hit a customer's parked car. No one saw me. I dented the front fender, quickly drove mine back into the bin and washed it again, hoping the customer would drive away in the meantime without noticing. He saw the dent, but I denied knowing anything about it.

I hosed the lot down, ran errands, vacuumed the cars, often washed up to thirty cars in one day only to have a late afternoon rain dirty them all again, making them ready for my repeated washings the following day. I took the abuse of the mechanics, and finally quit after one episode, when two salesmen had given me money to buy their lunch at a Mexican restaurant down the street. I brought back the two hot plates of green enchiladas. I carried them on a heavy tray, walked up the stairs of the office hut, waited for one of them to open the door. My hands were full with the hot plates. I called and called, but they just sat in the office and chatted. I reached for the door and the enchiladas fell to the pavement, the dishes shattering, the entire crew of salesmen laughing at me while I hosed the green sauce away. The two who sent me made my father pay for their lunch. He yelled at me because he was always broke, and often went without lunch because he had no money in his pockets. My summers of working as a lot boy taught me the art of conning the public, the craft of survival among desperate men.

◆ ◆ ◆

One night in San Elizario in my early twenties, I met a black woman who spoke fluent Spanish, a woman with the six kids and a refrigerator full of Carta Blanca beer cans and half-empty bottles of Pepsi. Her kids huddled in the tiny living room watching *The Wizard of Oz* on TV while I made love to her in the bedroom. She told me she wasn't being a whore, but she reminded me of the high school initiation at The Cave, the most notorious whorehouse in Juarez, where the *putas* wore black lipstick and black eye make-up, and painted their fingernails black, all of them voluptuous and wanting as they took us into the deeper caverns, gave us the electric shock of growing up on the border, threw us laughing into the streets, high school kids stumbling drunk on the way back to the bridge, laughing and joking to hide the incredible fear of falling into the endless cave whose depth we would not discover until our future years as grown men. The black woman of San Elizario was different, gentle and kind. She wanted me to stay with her. I forgot her name, but left ten dollars on the kitchen table for her kids and went home in the hot July night and never did anything like that again, because Dorothy and the Cowardly Lion kept coming back to me every time I wanted to cross the bridge into Juarez and go looking for enslaved women in the electric border city that pulled you down, sold you watered-down tequila, turned you over to the *Federales* if you didn't behave, if you weren't a proper drunk or whoremonger among them.

◆ ◆ ◆

When the Spanish conquered the pueblos, the friars responded to the killing and plundering by sticking giant crosses into the ground so that the people could come out of their huts and greet their new god, repent to the new savior. Some of the people climbed the wooden crosses and decorated them with colorful beads, feathers, and tiny replicas of the proud wolf, coyote, and bear. The friars watched them huddle around the crosses, whispered to each other constantly about their task of converting the heathen. It would be easier because these people recognized the cross by touching it, decorating it, accepting it into the village, acting as if their earlier fears and bloody resistance were the work of the devil, the animal in the form of dust storms and rattlesnakes that got in the way of the conquistadores. The desert wind tried to blow down the crosses from where they stood, embedded for pueblo people to see and crawl to pray below the wooden shadows as the Sangre de Cristo mountains turned a red color the people had never seen before.

◆ ◆ ◆

There are mountains I have never climbed, a flash of Rio Grande I have never crossed, a shadow of canyon I have never entered, a setting sun I have ignored in the red sky too many times. The hot wind from Chihuahua makes it hard to breathe. The pueblo people believe air and breathing are prayers. Air is the giver of life; it is a deity. The hot air of the desert makes it difficult to accept life here; it is hard on the lungs and the heart, making it troublesome to run across the sand dunes. As I breathe, I believe in *El Spirito de la tierra*, the prophetic drunkard drunk on desert rain. He is the old friend who visits me while this memory fever recovers from the encounter with the El Paso air.

◆ ◆ ◆

We hike to the graveyard on the hill above Cloride, a ghost town. We follow the path after exploring the old shacks. Wire crosses and cracked markers sink in the weeds. We stare at the fading inscriptions: Francisco Ramirez, 1878–1894. Killed by Apaches. Gabriela Castro, 1842–1871. Died in childbirth. I look cautiously into the trees as the hot breeze blows over us. Wordlessly, we wander among the dead, walk over the grave markers, spend minutes staring at each. Juan Somoza, 1837–1881. Killed by the Texas Rangers. In New Mexico? What were they doing here? Had they really come this far to get another Mexican? I kick dirt on the marker and at my solitude, wait for us to walk out of our trance, as if we were survivors when we really didn't know anything about this land that took these people and left the crumbling buildings as the larger cemetery that will never fade. As we leave the plots, I pick a tiny yellow flower from the weeds, set it gently at an infant's grave. Ester Silva, 1889–1890. No other words.

◆ ◆ ◆

Ruins of the white church look miniature at the bottom of the hill, a moment of prayer before the ghost town. You point to the vulture circling the green and open your book of North American birds. My friend, you come from the East and I want to point out my own birds. I remain quiet because the stillness of the day speaks for me the way the corral lines the daisies, the way we listen to the ponderosa pines as we descend into the valley. A brown and white hawk hunts across the sky. Tell me what kind. We hike deeper into the canyon, the stream a ribbon through the shadows. My pants and shoes are soaked, but you choose to

leap across. Under the red sandstone, you say you can't believe where you are. I bend and drink the cold water. A red
horned toad skips near my hand, layers of old skin peeling
off its back. We tell each other to listen. It is so quiet, I am
afraid. Blades of cactus click in a gentle breeze. We move
from the spot. I find the bleached leg bone of a cow. We rest
in the haze of a wooden cave. The tree sags with age, tiny
yellow apples strewn in the dirt. I pound the ground with
the bone, then throw it into the creek. Farther up, you find
the thigh bone of a deer, bullet holes cracked in it. The
quick cry of a hidden bird makes you stuff the bone into
your pack. You point to a mountain bluebird, the first I have
ever seen. Walking toward the bird's unclaimed horizon, I
count the length of our silence, over and over again.

✦ ✦ ✦

Out of the mist into the ghost dance, we hurl ourselves
over a winding road, caught by the exploding fog against
the red cliffs, and enter the haunted valley of Lincoln, New
Mexico, the famous town where Billy the Kid was briefly
imprisoned. He broke out of jail, killed two men, and left
bullet holes in the walls so the town could bring in tourist
dollars a century later. A lone wooden shack sits under the
trees, hypnotized and lost with this history and killing,
snowy hills rolling in their color. Approaching the old historical buildings we pass a Spanish *torreon,* its cracking
walls a little tower against the silent Apache, the silence of
being caught alive under cottonwoods and pines. We walk
along the banks of the Rio Bonito. I wonder where the cat-
tlemen died in the Lincoln County War, a Western shootout
at a time when the last Apaches and Commanches were falling from their horses, tumbling from the cliffs so the cowboys could be free to kill each other over cattle, the rail-

roads, money, and women. Bullet holes in the walls lead to the staircase of death in the courthouse.

Did these outlaws dream what we dream? Did they dream about snakes, or were they too busy dreaming about the torn saddle and the empty revolver, the brand sizzling on the cattle flanks, the old horse slipping out of its saddle to gallop beyond their dying dreams? Did they count how many Indians and Mexicans they killed for no reason? Why do so many Western monuments glorify outlaws? In N. Scott Momaday's novel *The Ancient Child* (Harper Perennial, 1989), an Indian writer takes the Billy the Kid myth and turns it into something his people, or any reader, is supposed to admire. The characters run through muddy streets. The Indian woman's breasts and hips burst out of her blouse and tight jeans, Momaday's description of her symbolizing the Western myth gone haywire. One of our best Native American writers reinvents the legend of Billy the Kid to fit the times. These old walls crack with newer bullet holes as I drop the book, jump in the car, and leave the haunted valley forever.

◆ ◆ ◆

The Bradys lived down the street and were the most racist boys I ever encountered—Joel, Roy, and Bobby torturing me from the eight grade through high school. Bobby, my age, was the master racist who constantly called me "dumb Mexican" and "greaser," always referring to me by the name of "Chuey." He was a track star at our high school and we rode to school in the mornings together. We started out as friends, but as the high school years went by, we drew apart. He had become a white supremacist by the time we graduated. His bully tactics, his meanness, and his punches were just enough to taunt me. He never really assaulted me, except verbally. I have not seen him in twenty-three years, but realize I had found a way to get back at him when we were sophomores. I managed to convince Gary Johnson, a guy I went to elementary school with, that Bobby was saying bad things about him. They did not really know each other, but they were always bragging as many high school toughs like to do. Somehow, a challenge to fight was made and Gary beat the crap out of Bobby. It happened at the park near my mother's house, a group of boys watching the bloody fight. I thought Bobby would win, but Gary surprised me. I will never forget how I helped Bobby to his feet, his face a bloody mess. We went to my house where he washed up. I don't recall what he said about the fight, but the distance between us grew wider. Only recently have I admitted to setting up this revenge against the one person who truly made my teenage life miserable. I found a way to get back at him for his cruelty toward me. I will never forget the remarks he made at me, year after year. I will never forget the hatred the Bradys showed me as we grew up. Most of all, I will never forget the power of young revenge.

◆ ◆ ◆

The scorpion season: The small red one jumps on my window screen. Its flashing motion is the quickness of every scorpion that has crossed my foot, one of the largest ones almost getting me when I sat on my bed, sometime during my high school years. It passed my bare toes without striking. I happened to look down at that moment, pausing from writing in my journal, and jumped back onto the bed to get away from it. Its appearance was a sign of unpredictable things, invisible motions bringing its tail to penetrate the body like a thorn come alive, a fang springing from the rattle, a majestic dance the scorpion performs as the fastest creature of the desert.

This late-night visitor was a pale red, instead of the normal straw color. What did it mean? Scorpions adopt the color of their surroundings. Why did this one camouflage itself red? Where was the blood, the redness of a hidden strike at the heart? When the scorpion sprang onto my window screen, the cool desert night settled over its movements and it clung to the wire. I turned off my lamp to find out if it was true. It glowed in the dark for an instant, then I couldn't see it. Its flame was alive for a split second. Years later, a friend told me scorpions can glow under ultraviolet light. Once he encountered several of them in the desert while camping, his expedition to study various species of cactus turning into the discovery that scorpions glow in the dark. Their wild shapes formed light patterns that constantly changed as he tried to stay out of their way, wondering if he would be safe in his sleeping bag that night. I turned on my light again. The red scorpion was gone, a spontaneous drop of blood leaving its aura to fade through the miniature holes of the window.

◆ ◆ ◆

A certain kind of desert madness got us through the years when we had to pass from isolated childhood to the carefree decade of wanting it all, thinking we could get by with not caring, pushing our lives as young writers beyond what we thought we knew. It was very simple when Jay Williams, one of the best fiction writers in the university writing program, came by the house on the river to ask a favor of Gary and me. He had a girlfriend from Columbia waiting in Juarez. She had no papers and had to cross illegally. We sat on our porch, drinking and reciting poems, the candles on the table marking our location. Jay talked us into helping her get across. He drove back to Juarez.

We waited for almost two hours, paced along the dark canal as several Border Patrol cars went by. We looked across the Rio Grande toward the shacks of the *colonia* across the water and spotted Jay's headlights. He turned them off as his girlfriend waded, carefree, across the low river. There was no Border Patrol car in sight as she walked calmly across the canal gates and joined us. She couldn't speak English. I don't recall her name, but her South American Spanish was difficult to understand. She sat with us, enjoying the cool evening along the river as we waited for Jay to drive back to this side. An hour later, he pulled up at the same instant as two Border Patrol cars went by the levee road. Jay thanked us many times.

◆ ◆ ◆

In the midst of recalling it, the idealism of a strong family comes down to how we are sustained and fed, the regular Sunday drives to the tamale factory in Ysleta one of the ways to keep the ideal concept alive. We went in my father's 1955 Ford sedan, my sister Pat and I toddlers who loved to stand on the car seats as we headed on the big adventure, my father and mother in the front seat. The drive to Ysleta in the lower valley was a long trip for me. There is the lingering smell of wonderful tamales mixed with the fear of being left in the car while my parents went into the store to buy them. Why did they leave us, a three- and four-year-old, alone in the car? The Ford is parked down the street from the store and I see my parents disappear around the corner. The smell of tortillas and tamales surrounds me. I thought I was being abandoned in the midst of overpowering odors and hunger. They always came back with bags of tamales and we headed home, but I wanted to go inside with them, wanted to see how they made the tamales so I could stop feeling afraid.

✦ ✦ ✦

We never went drinking in Juarez after that. It was in La Mano Blanca *cantina* near the *mercado* on a hot June night. The place was packed with *vaqueros* and a few *gringos* from El Paso. We sat drinking cheap bottles of Superior, the three of us celebrating the end of the school semester, three lost graduate students not knowing what to do next. We sat there getting drunk, listening to the loud conversations in Spanish, wondering what had made us go into this bar for the first time. He appeared out of the electric mist of the lights over the bar. The thin *vato* looked ill, with dirty black hair and nasty cuts all over his arms. He grabbed a chair and sat at our table without invitation. For a few seconds, we pretended he wasn't there. He held his arms out. We got a good look at the fresh, bleeding slashes on his arms. In Spanish he muttered, "I just got out of the Juarez jail. They did this to me." He was drunk and his red eyes danced in a fatalistic trance. The three of us—Jeff, Gary, and I—stared at each other as he squeezed one of his bleeding wounds with his fingers. The blood dripped onto our table. All three of us stood at once, pushed our full bottles of Superior toward him and bolted out without saying anything, practically running the twenty blocks to the international bridge to El Paso.

✦ ✦ ✦

You pray to the desert to stop raining because you are caught in a flash flood, your car stuck on a low road near the park by Cottonwood Springs. You can't get it started and the water is rushing faster down the *arroyos*, the sudden storm crashing and tearing across the Franklin Mountains, its black clouds hammering with clear lightning, the car starting to move on its own. You try to start the engine again, wondering if it would be better to force the door open and run. The muddy river slams against the car and pushes it a few feet toward the edge of the road. The car starts as the tallest wave you have ever seen in the desert rolls down the arroyo, but slows before reaching you. You manage to drive the car onto the highway, limbs of torn mesquite pounding against it. You swerve onto the road and watch the sea even itself miles down the cold, black hills of the desert, the rain whistling like bullets against your windshield.

◆ ◆ ◆

The adobe ruins finally disappeared years after I quit walking through them. They were in a field in the Upper Valley, on the back road to Las Cruces. They looked like old migrant-worker huts, rows of broken walls and caved-in roofs. I loved to walk into the rooms, kick tumbleweeds out of the way as I found old car tires, beer cans, and graffiti on the walls. The adobe ruins drew me inside whenever I drove alone in the area, but I never stopped to explore them with any of my friends. Once, as I stood in the middle of a dirt floor, I thought I heard someone whispering in the other room. I climbed over fallen beams and entered the adjoining area. There was nothing there expect tall piles of tumbleweeds. I heard the whispering again and a baby's cry. I stepped out into the bright sun of a cool October. A rusted school bus sat in the field a few yards away. I walked past several open doorways, then stopped in front of a tiny room. As I looked in, I spotted the white drawings on the far wall. Crude stick figures of a man, woman, and child were spray-painted on the hard mud. I stepped in and could

smell the fresh paint. Someone had been here not long ago.
I heard the whispering again, went outside the same instant
that a rotting beam fell behind me. It scared me and I ran to
my car. I paused. There was no one around. The ruins were
still coming apart, were still waiting for me to step back into
them at the right moment of habitation, at the instant when
I returned to the floor where families who gave birth to
their sons stood proudly the way those painted figures stood
on the cracked walls of their home.

✦ ✦ ✦

Memory fever comes from breathing in and out of my
hands, of taking my palms and watching the sweat glisten
upon them as I return from a long, desert hike. A cure for
the fever comes from the earliest memory I have. It is 1953.
I am a year old and my grandmother is lying on her bed. She
is taking care of me. I don't know where my mother is. It is
time to go to sleep, but my grandmother is playing with me.
She lies on her back, lifts me in one hand, and holds me in
the air above her. With her arm outstretched, she laughs,
pretends I am a toy airplane she can wave in an arc. I am a
year old and giggling, flying through the shadows thrown by
the votive candles she lights each night. She says something
I can't understand. I fly again, until she tires of the game
and sets me down to sleep. It is the sleep of an infant getting used to the rush of desert air, my flight above the candles a falling arc set by those who came before I was born.

The memory fever is the manifestation of life; it allows
me to go back to the arroyos, the canyons, the clusters of
cactus. I know the rattlesnake and lizard wait for the next
dream where, together, we can reveal the truth about El
Paso behind our *cuentos,* re-examine why we climbed the
cross to cut down those colorful beads, why we had to cross

the muddy Rio Grande a thousand times to find the wet adobe house steaming in the rain, someone to open the low wooden door and whisper an air of life, hold up an air of hands against the hot, unforgiving desert sun, wait for the *familia* huddled inside to stoke the fire and set the empty bowls before the table.

ABOUT THE AUTHOR

Ray Gonzalez is a poet, essayist, and editor born in El Paso, Texas. In addition to *Memory Fever,* he is the author of five books of poetry, including *Cabato Sentora* (1999) and *The Heat of Arrivals* (1996). The latter received a 1997 PEN/Oakland Josephine Miles Book Award for Excellence in Literature. He is also the editor of eleven anthologies, most recently *Muy Macho: Latino Men Confront Their Manhood* and *Touching the Fire: Fifteen Poets of Today's Latino Renaissance.* He has served as Poetry Editor for the *Bloomsbury Review* for seventeen years and recently founded a new poetry journal, *LUNA.* His awards include a 1998 Fellowship in Poetry from the Illinois Arts Council, a 1993 Before Columbus Foundation American Book Award for Excellence in Editing, and a 1988 Colorado Governor's Award for Excellence in the Arts. He currently holds the McKnight Land Grant Professorship at the University of Minnesota in Minneapolis.

WORKS BY RAY GONZALEZ

Essays and Memoirs
Memory Fever: A Journey Beyond El Paso del Norte
Turtle Pictures

Poetry
Apprentice to Volcanos
Cabato Sentora
From the Restless Roots
The Heat of Arrivals
Railroad Face
Twilights and Chants

Anthologies
After Aztlan: Latino Poets of the Nineties
City Kite on a Wire: 38 Denver Poets
Crossing the River: Poets of the Western U.S.
Currents from the Dancing River: Contemporary Latino
    Fiction, Nonfiction, and Poetry
Inheritance of Light
The Midnight Lamp
Mirrors Beneath the Earth: Short Fiction by Chicano Writers
Muy Macho: Latino Men Confront Their Manhood
Touching the Fire: Fifteen Poets of Today's Latino Renaissance
Under the Pomegranate Tree: The Best New Latino Erotica
Without Discovery: A Native Response to Columbus

Journals
The Guadalupe Review
LUNA: A New Journal of Poetry